The Healthy Faith-Building
CHURCH

The Healthy Faith-Building
CHURCH

Constructing Change in Changing Times

Pastor James R. Jones, Jr.
Doctor of Ministry

THE HEALTHY, FAITH-BUILDING CHURCH

Cover Design by Atinad Designs

© Copyright 2009

SAINT PAUL PRESS, DALLAS, TEXAS
First Printing, 2009

All rights reserved. No part of this publication may be reproduced, stored in a retrieval system, or transmitted in any form or by any means, electronic, mechanical, photocopying, recording, or otherwise, without the prior permission of the copyright owner, except for brief quotations included in a review of the book.

Unless otherwise stated, all Scripture quotations are from the New Revised Standard Version of the Holy Bible.

The name SAINT PAUL PRESS and its logo are registered as a trademark in the U.S. patent office.

ISBN-13: 978-0-9819672-9-5

Printed in the U.S.A.

This book represents a practical ministry doctoral project and is dedicated to the Church of Jesus Christ, God's hope for the world.

CONTENTS

Introduction...11

Chapter 1: Vision, Mission, and Core Values........................17

Chapter 2: Pastoral Leadership.....................................37

Chapter 3: The Church's Worship Life...............................57

Chapter 4: Small Groups and Discipleship...........................79

Chapter 5: Evangelism..99

Chapter 6: Ministry and Missions..................................129

Chapter 7: Fellowship...147

Chapter 8: The Healthy 21st Century Church.......................159

The Main Ingredient of a Truly Healthy Faith-Building Church......*169*

Introduction

I love the church. In my view, no other organization on the face of the earth has a greater mission. Unfortunately, many churches in North America and Europe are failing to meet their God-given purpose of making new disciples for Jesus Christ. While the church is called to grow believers, Jesus made it clear that He came for the lost and that His ministry focus was people far from God. I say this in love, but the truth is that some churches could care less about those who are lost. In Luke 18:8, Jesus asks a penetrating question for the ages: *"When the Son of Man comes, will he find faith on earth?"* Church, it is up to us. If we don't point the way to Jesus in this generation, who will? The time has come and the mission is clear: we must be a healthy faith-building church in these changing times or we will fail to win the next generation to Jesus Christ.

The major goal of this project is to show how the church can be healthy in its ministry and mission to build a Christ-grounded faith in both believers and non-believers in these changing times. In order to diagnose and prescribe a solution to the church's failing health, I will take a look at the following: (1) the vision, mission and core values of churches; (2) pastoral leadership, (3) the worship life of congregations, (4) small group and discipleship experiences, (5) evangelism and faith-sharing emphases, (6) ministry and mission opportunities and (7) building community through fellowship. By constructing and implementing healthy disciplines in these seven areas of church life, congregations can build a Christ-grounded faith in the lives of both believers and non-believers in these challenging times we face.

Sadly, some modern day churches have lost their sense of vision and core values. Proverbs 29:18 says, *"Where there is no vision, the people perish"* (KJV). A church that ceases to reach out and win the lost for Jesus Christ is a congregation that has lost its sense of our Lord's mission for believers. In his groundbreaking book titled *The Purpose Driven Church*, author and pastor, Rick Warren laments: "Many churches are barely surviving because they have no vision…"[1]

A church cannot be a healthy organization without a clear sense of its vision, mission, and core values. Moreover, a church must also have effective pastoral leadership in order to reach the lost in a new century. As we shall see, a healthy church must be led by a pastor who is committed to staying in one setting for a long period of time. Churches that change pastors every few years can virtually guarantee that they will not experience long-term growth and health. In addition, local church pastors should pledge to be honing their skills and taking care of their personal lives during these changing times. Leaders of healthy churches should also practice setting firm boundaries in order to keep themselves sharp for the Lord's work.

And, as worship leaders, pastors must be sure to commit themselves to see that services are carried out with a focus on

Jesus Christ and excellence. Holy Spirit-led worship should include uplifting music and a culturally relevant message that touches the hearts of people and leads them into ministry. Moreover, worship must be supplemented by healthy small group ministries that include teaching, hospitality to newcomers, member care, mission opportunities for small group members, and fellowship that binds small group participants together. Healthy churches in the new century should also practice creative and cutting- edge evangelism that is exercised at the personal, small group, and church-wide levels. A focus on constantly drawing people to the feet of Jesus should lead the evangelism efforts of such congregations. And, just as in Acts 1:8, Jesus called the disciples into ministry in Jerusalem (local), Judea (regional) and Samaria (worldwide), so we too must maintain ministry and mission at these three levels. Finally, healthy churches will be communities where fellowship thrives. Congregations that enjoy being together in Christian fellowship attract newcomers to the faith and create vital congregations.

As I undertake this important reflection on the church's life and health, I realize that I owe many thanks to some great friends of Jesus. First, I want to thank my grandparents for their awesome God-inspired influence over my life. Without the prayers and nurture of my grandparents, I would certainly not have been able to complete the work before you. Furthermore, I want to thank my parents for being patient, caring, and loving me as I developed. Lord knows it was not always easy for them. But, they did a great job teaching me about my Christian responsibilities. I also want to thank my brother. We enjoyed many good laughs together and an occasional round of golf. Like me, my brother, Mike, has come a long way in his faith journey. May God go with him the rest of the way. Moreover, I also have some wonderful aunts and uncles who have nurtured me in the faith. They have all enriched my experiences with our Lord Jesus Christ. Finally, I want to thank my wife, Lynn, and our son, Caleb. Our son, nearly eight now, can scarcely imagine what God has in store for his life. He is a true joy and reminds me every day of how much it cost God to give up His only Son…there is no greater love than that.

Finally, I want to thank the faithful people of the United Methodist Church for giving me a place to serve God. I was ordained an elder in the church in 1995. My first parish was a two church charge near Winston-Salem, North Carolina. I was an inexperienced pastor when I drifted their way. I appreciate them putting up with me and teaching me the ropes those first three years. In 1998, I took a pastoral position in North Georgia at a small church called, Bethlehem, in Buford. Truly, they were some of the finest people that I have ever met. If it were not for their love and care, I probably would not even be in the ministry today. Next, I was fortunate enough to move a few miles north of Buford and serve at Gainesville First United Methodist Church as their associate pastor. It was there that I grew in my ministerial experience and felt called to do great things for Christ. I will always be indebted to my friends there. Later, from 2006-2008, I was blessed to serve Christ with the great people of Riverside Park United Methodist Church in Jacksonville, Florida. It is a beautiful historic church located near downtown. These people were kind enough to give me a church home in Florida. Words cannot adequately express my sincere appreciation for their love. And, finally, now I find myself as Servant Ministries Pastor at Beach United Methodist

Church in Jacksonville Beach, Florida. With dynamic leadership and a large following, Beach is challenging me to do awesome things for God's kingdom. The current lead pastor, Jerry Sweat, says that excellence honors God and inspires people. I could not agree more. To God be the glory.

—James R. Jones, Jr.
January 2009

Chapter I

VISION, MISSION AND CORE VALUES

VISION DEFINED

Leadership expert, Burt Nanus, opens his book, *Visionary Leadership* with the following sentence: "There is no more powerful engine driving an organization toward excellence and long-range success than an attractive, worthwhile, and achievable vision of the future, widely shared."[1] In the Bible, Jesus shares a critical vision for the early church in Matthew 28:19-20: *"Go therefore and make disciples of all nations, baptizing them in the name of the Father and of the Son and of the Holy Spirit, and teaching them to obey everything that I have commanded you."* Successful people, businesses and churches are all driven by a passionate vision. So, what is vision? Author and pastor, Craig Miller, writes that vision "is the navigation system that tells direction."[2]

A year and a half ago, I took a student ministries group on a summer mission trip to Tampa, Florida. We met another

.udent ministries group there while we were on the trip. Their church had just purchased a new GPS system for their bus. One afternoon, guided by their GPS system, we followed them in our church van and ended up in the parking lot of a shopping center rather than the beachside park where we were headed. If your church has the wrong vision, or the navigational route to your destination, you too, can end up in the wrong place. Even more so, if your church has no vision at all, then how in the world will you go anywhere! I serve on a church staff with another pastor who is blind. I would never even think of asking her to drive me anywhere (and, she certainly would not offer!) Churches that are led by leaders with no vision are like people who are being driven to a location by someone who is blind. No one wants to do that!

THE CHARACTERISTICS OF A HEALTHY VISION

The first characteristic of a healthy vision is that it is large, attractive or unlimited in scope. Notice Jesus' unique vision for the church in Matthew 28:19-20: *"Go therefore and make disciples of all nations, baptizing them in the name of the Father and of the Son and of the Holy Spirit, and teaching them to obey everything that I have commanded you."* That's a large vision! That is a vision that is attractive because it empowers disciples to multiply and make new disciples. And, notice that Jesus calls us out of our geographic comfort zones. We may feel comfortable talking to our local friends and neighbors about Jesus and inviting them to church. However, Jesus' vision calls us out of our culturally insulated neighborhoods to the highways and byways of life. We are called to get on a plane and share Christ overseas. We are called to share Christ with people in other regions of the United States. We are called to be His hands and feet everywhere, no matter where the roads and skies might take us.

It is simple. People like being part of something big. Unfortunately, some churches and other organizations don't have a large, attractive vision with an unlimited scope. Some parishes are content with merely having a vision that meets the needs of their own members rather than those desires of the community. Shame on them! Jesus said that He came for the "lost" and that the "sick" were at the top of His agenda. Is that true for your church? Is that true for your ministry? A large attractive vision of any organization that meets the needs and wants of those in one's community will touch hearts and lives. For example, think of Walt Disney's business vision. He transformed acres of central Florida wasteland into a magnificent amusement park that attracts people from all continents. Perhaps, your thinking is too limited for your church setting. God may be calling you to do something mighty rather than mediocre. God may be calling you to do something that makes the front page of your city's newspaper rather than the back pages of your church newsletter. In the book of Exodus, God called Moses to lead and release the Israelites from slavery. What if Moses had only decided to lead and release only one slave when God called him to break the bondage for all God's people? God is calling the church to do great things in these changing times so it is up to us to have a large, attractive vision that is unlimited in scope.

The second characteristic of a healthy vision is that it is realistic or pragmatic. In other words, while an organization or church must have a large and attractive vision, it must also

.chievable. If the vision is all fluff and no substance, people will gradually lose interest. If the vision is so large that people cannot possibly achieve it, they will throw up their hands and quit. The vision must be achievable or the people in the church will think the pastor has lost his or her mind. Several years ago, I served on a church staff where the lead pastor would periodically throw out virtually unachievable visions. When he first came to the church, he insisted that the church should be able to grow five times its size in the first year. Unfortunately, the church was located in a small community with no through street and had not grown in years. In addition, people did not share the pastor's vision for growth and he presented no plan for making it happen. The result? You guessed it. One year later, our church was about the same size as the previous year. A vision that is unrealistic and unachievable does not motivate followers. People are not motivated by what they think they cannot achieve; rather, they are motivated by what they think they can achieve. Moreover, when a pastoral leader introduces a vision that is impractical, he or she loses credibility with followers. And, leaders who lose credibility may lose the opportunity to move people toward any future subsequent vision, even if it is achievable.

The third characteristic of a healthy vision is that it should be creative and imaginative. Nowadays, creativity and imagination count! Once upon a time, churches could open their doors on Sunday morning and people flocked to the pews. Not anymore! It takes creative and imaginative skill for churches to touch their neighborhoods now. Churches and church leaders are challenged now more than ever to discover a vision that is creative and imaginative enough to touch the hearts of people in their community and transform lives. I recently read an article about a church in South Florida that was having a problem with teenage vandals striking their church and destroying property. After several incidents of vandalism, the church began to seek the guidance of the Holy Spirit about how to deal with these young people. The result? The church literally opened its doors to these teenagers on Friday nights. Church members played games with the teenagers and some of the older members served as "mentors" and listened to them as they shared their struggles. Oh, and guess what? The vandalism problems stopped. The church renewed its vision for reaching the "lost teenagers" in its community and protected its property simultaneously. That is what you call a win-win for the kingdom of God! And, that is just one example of a creative and imaginative vision for reaching one's church community.

Has your church lost its fire and enthusiasm for its vision? Then, perhaps it is time to reformulate your vision. Just as a computer shuts down and has to reboot, perhaps your church needs to "reboot" its vision. A vision that is bland and lifeless is a vision that is dead. And, a dead church nowadays is on a dead-end to nowhere. So, what separates your church from the one down the street? Is your church's vision compelling and creative? Or, maybe an even better question is: do you even know what your church's vision is? Sadly, some churches and pastors have no idea what vision God is calling them to. The result is death. Remember Proverbs 29:18? *"Where there is no vision, the people perish"* (KJV). When people don't know where they are headed, you had better believe that they are bound to get there.

The fourth characteristic of a healthy vision is that it must be future oriented. In short, a vision looks ahead. Just as your look ahead to help you see where you are going, a vision looks ahead to help an organization see where it is going. Once again, at the conclusion of Matthew's gospel, as Jesus is preparing to leave the disciples, He tells them to *"go... make disciples of all nations."* Jesus is pointing ahead to future events. Likewise, churches and church leaders must peer into the future when they construct a vision. A vision that merely states the church's purpose is no vision at all. A vision looks forward into the future toward something that has not yet been achieved. In 2002, I had a vision that God was calling me to start a new church. I had a dream one night, and in it, I strongly felt God's call upon my life to plant a new church. Seven years later, as I type these words, I am still looking forward to that opportunity. I recently confirmed with a key person in church leadership that I have been chosen to start a new church. While I will not plant the church with a team of people for two or three more years, I could tell you now some basics about the church's vision and life.

Vision is always looking forward towards the church's future. Churches that only focus on the past and present are doing themselves and God a great disservice. Biblical people are called to look into the future. For example, in the midst of intense persecution and untold suffering, John envisions a future new Heaven and earth in Revelation 21:1: *"Then I saw a new heaven and a new earth; for the first heaven and first earth had passed away, and the sea was no more."* God gave that New Testament prophet the ability to look into the future. Stop what you are doing right now. Pause for just a moment. And, in the stillness of this moment, ask God to help you and your church leaders craft a vision for your church's future. Right now, don't focus on the past and present. Simply allow God to give you a vision of the future and be challenged with the Spirit's response to your prayer.

A fifth characteristic of a healthy vision is that it is grounded in God's Word. It is a given but must be stated nevertheless. We are called to place our visions on the foundation of God's Word. In Luke 6:48, Jesus says that someone who hears and acts on His words are like a man who builds his house on a strong foundation which is capable of handling severe storms. Likewise, a healthy vision for one's church must be absolutely grounded in scripture. If a church's vision is pastor-centered or fad-driven, then it will only last for a short time. You may have heard of churches that fizzled out or declined after the pastor stepped down from leadership. Such a church was built around the pastor's strong authoritarian leadership or personality. However, other churches have survived a pastoral transition because they had a larger sense of God's vision based upon the unchanging Word of God.

Imagine for a moment that a new student is learning to drive a car but has never read a driver's manual. That uninformed student will struggle and is more likely to have an accident than someone else who has read a driver's manual and passed a driver education course. Healthy churches have healthy visions that are based upon a healthy interpretation of scripture. If a church's vision is not consistent with scriptural mandates, then it is a human organization, not a living organism that is transforming lives for Christ.

The final characteristic of a healthy vision is that it is widely accepted by those who are called to follow it. If a vision is only held by the pastoral leader or church staff, then it is bound to fail. If a vision is only held by a small group within the church, then it is doomed from the start. On the other hand, a vision that is generally accepted by many in the church will transform both the body of believers themselves and the community itself.

Several years ago, when I was the pastor of a small church outside of Atlanta, Georgia, our congregation was struggling to find a ministry vision. So, for the better part of one afternoon, a key group of leaders sat in the historic church chapel and had some honest discussions with me about the church's future and its vision for ministry. As a result of that conversation, we established one of the most effective children's ministries in that area and the church began to show some significant spiritual and numerical growth. In fact, one official in our church's hierarchy told me that we had one of the best growth percentages in the entire area over a year's time.

I believe that one primary reason that our church moved forward during that time period was the vision was widely shared by many people. Now, that doesn't mean that one hundred percent of the church bought into the vision. In fact, one elderly woman told me that we were "neglecting" old people by focusing our vision on reaching lost children in the area. While I was polite but firm about our church's vision with the woman, I also felt a sense of satisfaction that our ministry was starting to make strong strides at that point in our church's life. No vision will be shared by everyone. However, a vision that is shared by no one is headed nowhere.

MISSION DEFINED

While vision has to do with the direction and future orientation of church life, mission is the "primary purpose for being."[3] In his book, *The Purpose Driven Church*, author and writer, Rick Warren, observes, "A clear purpose not only defines what we do, it defines what we do not do."[4] For churches, purpose deals with the issue, "What are we here for?" and "Why do we exist?" Unfortunately, many historical churches that have been around for years have both forgotten and outlived their purpose. These congregations merely exist to "take care of church members" or "care for each other." But, Jesus never intended for churches to merely exist for their own needs and desires. Rather, Jesus calls us out of our comfort zones to be in ministry with the "lost sheep of Israel."

THE CHARACTERISTICS OF A HEALTHY MISSION

The first characteristic of a healthy mission for a church is that it be Biblically grounded. In other words, a church's mission must be consistent with Christ's mission in scripture. Jesus often reveals His purpose in the gospels:
"I came that they may have life, and have it abundantly" (John 10:10).

"I came into this world for judgment so that those who do not see may see, and those who do see may become blind" (John 9:39).

"I have come as light into the world, so that everyone who believes in me should not remain in the darkness" (John 12:46).

The three verses above are just a sample of scriptures that unveil the purpose of Jesus. **In short, Jesus targets the "lost" and**

"those who live in darkness." Thus, any healthy church mission statement must include the purpose of evangelism, which means drawing lost souls into the body of Christ. Some church settings have become so exclusive and clannish that they have forgotten Christ's primary Biblical mission to reach the lost. The prescription for the church's disease of "membership myopia" involves reaching out to the ones who need to hear the good news of the gospel.

Tragically, some church's mission statements and ministries do not reflect the call to reach the lost. As a result, such churches will experience decline over time until they are no longer effective in their outreach. Due to deaths, transfer of members, moves, and other real life events, every church is subject to losing people. Therefore, churches that are not focused on reaching and assimilating newcomers will steadily decline over time until they effectively target the lost in their mission and ministries. On the other hand, some churches build their entire mission around reaching those who do not know Jesus. One of America's largest churches, Willow Creek in suburban Chicago, describes its mission statement succinctly: "To turn irreligious people into fully devoted followers of Jesus."[5] Pastor Bill Hybels points out that the church is fully devoted to their mission and strives to minister with excellence. Consequently, the church has grown to become one of the most effective churches in America at reaching the lost with the gospel of Jesus Christ.

A second trait of a healthy mission for a church is that it be specific. Rick Warren comments in *The Purpose Driven Church* that "a narrow mission is a clear mission."[6] If a church's mission is vague, then both the pastor and the church itself will not even know what they are trying to accomplish. Once, I was in a church meeting where the leadership team was gathered to discuss various ideas for community outreach. In the middle of the conversation, the pastor spoke up and acknowledged that the church did not have a clear sense of its own mission in that local community.

The truth is, if the pastor of the church does not know what its mission is, then how will its leadership team or the guest who walks through the doors? In the end, the church that tries to please everyone will please no one at all. At the time of this writing, my brother owns a mattress store. If you walked into his store and asked for a cheeseburger with fries, you would be sorely disappointed chewing on all that mattress foam. His mission is not to sell food. It is to sell mattresses. Churches should not apologize for not being a part of every "good" cause in their communities. Rather, they should find their unique contribution to making disciples and exploit it for all it is worth!

Again, the mission must be specific and have a target. A church that targets everyone will reach no one. And, a church that targets someone in particular will at least reach some for the kingdom of God. In a sense, when it comes to mission, less is more!

A third element of a healthy mission is to be transferable. Author and pastor, Rick Warren, writes that a mission statement should be "short enough to be remembered and passed on by everyone in your church."[7] A few years ago, the credit card company, Visa, had the mission motto "It's everywhere you want to be." Unfortunately, for many in credit card debt today, Visa is accepted at too many places that one wants to be! However, that short phrase was effective because it was memorable and summed up a key aspect of the company's mission—to have its credit card accepted and used in as many parts of the globe as possible.

If you ask the average church member the mission of their respective church, they probably would have a difficult time telling you. Most likely, you would hear a lot of "oh's" and "ah's." However, ask someone from an effective church its mission statement and you'll get an instant response! Those connected to an effective church are proud to be part of its mission in the local community. In essence, they are part of something larger than themselves when incorporated into a church that is living out mission. And, the fact that the church people share that mission statement with people in their communities makes it multiply that much more! Again, just as in targeting your mission, less is more. You can say a lot in a few words and still say much when summing up your church's mission statement. As the owner of a mattress store, my brother formulated a mission statement for his business: "Dedicated to a good night's sleep." If a mattress store has a transferable mission, shouldn't a church? I haven't seen my brother in three months and I know what his store is trying to accomplish. And, some church members sit on the pew every Sunday and have no idea what their church is about. How sad!

A final aspect of a church's mission is to be measurable. In my experience as a pastor, I have discovered that the church is often worse in this category than the other dimensions that I have discussed so far. Rick Warren challenges church leaders with this pointed question: "Will you be able to prove what you've accomplished at the end of each year?"[8] Businesses analyze their effectiveness by asking how much they accomplished at the end of the year. These businesses do detailed reports that show how much was sold and what their profit margins were.

However, in some church settings, when the question is asked, "How many disciples did we make this year?" people are aghast. Inevitably, some bring up the issue of "spiritual growth." Granted, spiritual growth is important in the lives of church folk. But, shouldn't that spiritual growth result in reaching out to others in the name of Jesus? A church dedicated to the exclusive spiritual growth of the "church family" is self-serving and out of touch with the greater need of its community. So, it is fair for church leaders to evaluate and ask, "How did we do with that this year?" Or, "How many new people did we reach for Jesus Christ this year?" Year-end evaluations might also include examining key large scale church events to see whether they have outlived their effectiveness. Too often, churches cling to ministries that are no longer reaching people in these changing times. Thus, such churches must take year-end "gut checks" to see whether certain ministries should continue. After all, why put your church's energy into ministries that are not reaching people for the Kingdom? Wouldn't your church be better served to spend your time doing things that really reach out into the neighborhood?

CORE VALUES DEFINED

In addition to having a sense of vision and mission for your local church, each congregation must also examine its core values. Craig Miller defines core values as "the bedrock beliefs and purposes that guide a congregation's decisions."[9] Just as mortar helps hold bricks together, so core values unite a congregation and help define who they are.

Miller asserts that "One's faith, understanding of scripture, experiences of God and traditions all go toward forming core values."[10] In my pastoral experience at one church, I noticed that history and tradition were the revered core values. The congregation strongly cared for its older and long-time members of the church. As a result, it was sometimes difficult to assimilate new people into that setting because they did not share the history and tradition with those who have been in the congregation for a while. Once, I had a discussion with someone who defined himself as a member who had just joined "recently." "How long ago did you join?" I asked. His response was, "eight years ago." I sensed that even after eight years he was just beginning to feel like a part of the church.

KEY CORE VALUES IN A CHANGING WORLD

Whether stated or unstated, all churches have core values. Core values have the advantage of giving church leaders and members a "filter through which we judge right and wrong, make choices and decisions, and evaluate our actions."[11] So, if a ministry or course of actions does not fit our set of core values then we do not follow through. However, if a leadership choice does fit our core values then we act on it.

The first critical core value that church leaders must practice in these changing times is teamwork. In the past, church leadership sometimes amounted to the pastor making a unilateral decision on behalf of the congregation. However, in today's world, pastors must make decisions within the framework of a church leadership team. A modern day pastor that leans towards autocratic and dictatorial decision making will either end up jobless or with a small congregation. Today's changing times demand that pastors work with a team of individuals toward realizing the vision and mission of the local church. In his book, *The Performance Factor: Unlocking the Secrets of Teamwork*, author, Pat MacMillan, identifies six characteristics of an effective team: "common purpose, crystal clear roles, accepted leadership, effective processes, solid relationships and excellent communication."[12] He observes that a "team leader must earn the acceptance of team members. The only boss of a team is the task."[13] Effective pastors in these changing times will be team leaders who seek to accomplish a task within a team environment.

Recently, my family took a trip to Universal Studios and Islands of Adventure in Orlando, Florida. At the time, my six-year-old son was a huge Spiderman fan. We rode an exciting thrill ride where Spiderman acts alone to fight the evil characters on the ride. At the conclusion of this mind-boggling ride, Spiderman has all the villains tied up in a web and has successfully completed his mission of defeating these evil characters. Pastoral leaders too often give in to the temptation to be superheroes in our church settings. Pastors may be tempted to fight the powers of evil themselves and even vilify others on the church leadership team. However, pastors should not give in to the "Spiderman" temptation. Nowadays, building faith in others means allowing them to be part of that critical process. As effective teams accomplish effective missions, the credit must be given to God, not to the pastor or even to the church leadership team. Such teams must be made up of people with differing abilities and gifts so that the body of Christ may be edified in our local settings. When the Corinthian church was arguing about who the most important leader in the church was, Paul reminded them in 1 Corinthians 3:6: *"I planted, Apollos watered, but God gave the growth."* In other words, the Apostle Paul was saying that it takes a team (not one individual) to build a church. When James and John battled over who would sit at Jesus' right hand, He reminded them true greatness was about humble teamwork, not exaltation.

In addition to teamwork, another core value for churches and leaders in a changing world is creativity.[14] In the book of Genesis, God created for six days straight. Genesis 1:25 reads: *"God made the wild animals of the earth of every kind, and the cattle of every kind, and everything that creeps upon the ground of every kind."* Let's face it. God is in the creating business.

Several years ago, my wife and I had the opportunity to visit the San Diego Zoo. I was absolutely blown away at the variety of animals. There were many types of animals that I recognized and others that I had never even heard of. It is obvious that God loves variety and is a creative artist. So, why aren't churches more creative? In fact, those outside the church tend to describe believers as being anything but creative. There are lots of ways to do church. In fact, the only basic Biblical outline for a worship service is found in Acts 2:42: *"They devoted themselves to the apostle's teaching and fellowship, to the breaking of bread and the prayers."* Those are the elements of a Biblical worship service. The rest is simply up to us. Go into some worship services on Sunday morning and you'll think that you've landed smack dab in the middle of a funeral. People look melancholy and messages are preached with little preparation and passion.

No wonder some church pews are empty! We certainly have to seek to be more creative about how we do worship, ministry, evangelism, discipleship, and fellowship. After all, this is the Lord's work so let's show some enthusiasm and planning in our ministries. Pastors, if you are not creative, find someone with that gift and make sure that he or she is an integral part of the leadership team. A church that is not creative in these changing times is a church that is headed for long-term failure.

Another essential core value in today's changing times for churches and leaders is character and integrity.[15] Character counts for leaders and leadership teams. The rise and downfall of many ministries can be traced to issues of character and integrity. Not long ago, there was a story in our local newspaper about a minister of a large thriving church in the area. The church had a successful television ministry and was growing by leaps and bounds. However, after the minister sent an explicit text message to several teenage girls in the church, outraged parents notified authorities and the media. The rest is history. The pastor resigned and at this writing, the church is still reeling from the fallout of his actions. Years of faithful ministry can be destroyed by a bad choice on the part of a church leader. And, the fact is, people are watching the church to make sure that its leaders walk the walk rather than talk the talk.

A few months ago, I had the opportunity to read Tony Dungy's book, *Quiet Strength*. Dungy is the former head coach for the NFL's Indianapolis Colts. In February 2007, he became the first African-American head coach to win a Super Bowl. However, Dungy is also known for his unwavering faith in God through Jesus Christ. He writes in his book, "I hired my staff with a few basic thoughts in mind. First, they had to be men of character and integrity."[16] Dungy knows how important character and integrity are in professional sports. Meanwhile, another NFL team, the Atlanta Falcons, were struggling that same year due to their quarterback's participation in an illegal dog fighting ring. Michael Vick, the Atlanta Falcon's quarterback in question, had to serve a prison sentence for his connection to the illegal dog fighting ring. Consequently, his team had one of its worst seasons on record. Character and integrity count, on and off the field.

SUMMARY

Vision, mission, and core values are extremely important for churches and church leaders. While vision refers to future direction and destination, an organization's mission has to do with its sense of purpose or reason for being. And, core values are the foundational beliefs and firm set of values that an organization must adhere to through thick and thin. Unfortunately, some churches and leaders have lost sight of Christ's vision for the church.

While Jesus calls us to make new disciples, some churches and leaders are simply content to take care of the sheep in the pen. Have we forgotten His vision for the church? And, have we lost sight of our purposes? In these changing times, healthy churches and leaders will have vision and mission characteristics that have been outlined in chapter one. And, without a strong sense of core values guiding the way, some churches and leaders are headed for doom unless they do a serious health check. But, there is hope for the church; hope that we as churches will return to our vision, mission, and core values with all the strength and vigor of the Holy Spirit to guide us.

Chapter 2

PASTORAL LEADERSHIP

While vision, mission, and core values are vital to a healthy church, it takes a strong leader to cast them as a congregation moves forward in ministry. In the first major section of chapter two, I will outline several key aspects of a healthy pastor's personal life: his or her faith, the importance of moral boundaries, solid Christian friendships, a servant-hearted attitude that considers others first, and the pastor's role as a spouse and parent. Second, I will take a look at the pastor's professional life with regard to the following areas: committing to the long haul at a given church, continuously improving his or her leadership ability, a servant paradigm for leadership, a thorough and objective examination of the pastor's weaknesses, and the importance of developing leaders in one's ministerial setting. Along the way, I will cite personal stories and examples that highlight the importance of all the above areas with respect to pastoral leadership.

THE PASTOR'S PERSONAL LIFE

Speaking as a pastor myself, it is important to distinguish the minister's personal life from his or her professional life. The New Testament clearly states that if the pastor's personal life is in shambles, then he or she is unfit to serve as a ministerial leader. Thus, it is extremely important to make a careful study of the pastor's personal life. In a sense, the pastor's personal faith, moral boundaries, friendships, attitude, and family life are all manifested for better or worse in one's professional life. Indeed, the pastor's personal life can and will have a significant impact on his or her professional life. And, it all begins with the pastor's faith.

Hebrews 11:6 says *"And without faith it is impossible to please God, for whoever would approach him must believe that he exists and that he rewards those who seek him."* Therefore, it is absolutely critical that a pastoral leader have a solid faith that is founded upon a personal relationship with Jesus Christ.

Authors, Andy Stanley and Stuart Hall, of North Point Community Church outside Atlanta, Georgia, observe that "Faith is confidence that God is who He says He is and that He will do all He has promised to do."[1] The pastor who does not have faith in God will please neither God nor his or her congregation. And, ultimately, the pastor without faith in Jesus Christ will be miserable in his or her calling to ministry. A healthy pastor of a healthy church is one who spends a lot of time on his or her knees in prayer. Jesus, Himself, exemplified this pattern of work and prayer in His own ministry. At critical times in His own ministry, Jesus spent personal time in prayer with God the Father. Too often, the pastoral leader is so busy attending to another's relationship with God that he or she fails to grow in his or her own relationship with God. The result is typically ministry "burn out" or worse yet, a loss of faith in

Jesus Christ. Just as a growing plant is nurtured by falling rain and fertilizer, so a pastoral leader's relationship with God becomes mature through prayer, scripture reading, journaling, retreats, and meeting with an accountability partner (these strategies will be discussed later in this chapter). On a daily basis, it seems like such a small thing for a minister to spend daily time in prayer, scripture reading and practicing the spiritual disciplines. However, the "seeds" of faith result in a great harvest to prepare the pastor for leadership in the local church.

Recently, I was thinking about how much time I spend in physical exercise and intentionally going to the gym. Even though I don't see a huge difference in my physical appearance from day to day, I realize that exercise has helped me to maintain good long-term health. And, the same is true of the spiritual practices that help build a pastor's faith. While one prayer, or one scripture reading may not seem to make much of a difference in a pastoral leader's life, ultimately he or she will benefit in his or her long-term relationship with God.

So, how does the pastoral leader maintain a healthy relationship with God? Prayer, scripture reading, journaling, retreats and meeting with an accountability partner are some practical examples of how to build one's faith in Jesus Christ. Author, Henri Nouwen, calls prayer the "furnace of transformation."[2] In scripture, Paul often writes about *"praying without ceasing"* and even points to the urgency and priority of prayer. As a believer, prayer involves both listening and speaking. Often, we are too busy or too attention deficit to listen as we pray. But, active prayer involves listening to the guidance of the Holy Spirit.

In addition to prayer, pastoral leaders must also engage in the reading of scripture. There are a variety of methods for reading scripture. In 2007, at the age of forty, I read through the entire Bible in one year. Often, that entailed reading several chapters per day. However, this year, I am reading the Bible one chapter and book at a time. As I do, I pray the scripture and ask God to reveal how it speaks to me that day. It is a deep and refreshing approach to daily scripture reading.

Journaling is another method of building one's personal faith. For some, journaling can be a healthy way to express one's innermost thoughts and feelings. When our spiritual desires and yearnings are put down on paper, it helps us to reflect on what is going on inside our souls.

Another method of deep spiritual reflection involves participating in a retreat. As a personal goal, I try to have at least one personal retreat per year where I focus attention on my relationship with God. Again, in scripture, Jesus, Himself, spends extended periods of time with God the Father. After His baptism, the Gospel of Matthew reports that Jesus spent forty days in the wilderness. Now that's a retreat!

Finally, pastoral leaders should also have an accountability partner with who to share their spiritual lives. For the last five years, I have had one. He is a pastor who lives nearby. We have a lot in common, yet we complement each other because we tend to each have a unique perspective on life and ministry. We laugh together, cry together, support each other, and pray without ceasing. In Luke 10: 1 and following, when Luke records the mission of the seventy, he notes that Jesus sends them out in "pairs." The truth is that we were not meant to serve God alone. Rather, we are offered the gift of spiritual companionship in the scriptures. Healthy pastors have healthy relationships with other disciples.

In addition to building faith by practicing the spiritual disciplines, Andy Stanley and Stuart Hall write that pastoral leaders and others must observe "moral boundaries."[3] Namely, in their book titled, *The Seven Checkpoints for Youth Leaders*, they argue that believers must practice moral boundaries with regard to the issue of sex. Many televangelists and other pastoral leaders in the last several years have failed in the area of sexual boundaries. An unhealthy sexual lifestyle is not only sweeping our nation, but our churches as well. And, unfortunately, some pastoral leaders have been guilty of making unwise choices with regards to sex. News of televangelists who have fallen from grace due to sexual misconduct is no stranger to newspaper headlines. And, even locally, many ministers are aware of other pastors who have fallen prey to their perverted sexual desires. The result is a loss of credibility for both pastoral leaders and the church as a whole. The scriptures constantly cite a believer's need to stay pure and spotless in the sight of Jesus. In the Sermon on the Mountain, Jesus challenges us to *"Be perfect, therefore, as your Heavenly Father is perfect"* (Matthew 5:48). In the last few weeks, several members of our church interviewed people in a local park about their viewpoints on the church and community. Unfortunately, several people who were interviewed expressed that they did not trust pastors and churches due to so much media publicity about moral indiscretions. In order to regain the trust of others, the church must heed Jesus' call to be perfect as our Heavenly Father is perfect.

Even as pastoral leaders practice setting good moral boundaries, Andy Stanley and Stuart Hall also recommend that they have "healthy friendships."[4] Proverbs 13:20 advises, *"Whoever walks with the wise becomes wise, but the companion of fools suffers harm."* Leadership can be lonely. So, pastoral leaders need to develop a network of relationships that help encourage their faith walk. The vicissitudes of ministry leadership will bring heartache, headaches, and emotional strain. Therefore, pastoral leaders need to share their thoughts and feelings with others. In some areas, pastors form local ministerial alliances where they can share friendships with other church leaders. And, in other settings, pastors simply need someone they meet with on a regular basis to have a listening ear. Pastors certainly should not expect their spouses and children to be their therapists! Rather, they should seek healthy friendships outside their families. Such healthy friendships not only help build the pastor's faith, but also reinforce the moral boundaries that ministerial leaders should set.

Beyond maintaining healthy friendships, pastoral leaders would also be wise to put "others first." Nowadays, the best way to lead is through service. Jesus advocated servant leadership in Matthew 23:11 when He said to the crowd and to His disciples, *"The greatest among you will be your servant."* For better or worse, pastors are visible figures in their communities. People are always observing pastoral leaders to study how they lead and respond to various situations. The bottom line is that pastors represent Jesus both on and off the job. A pastor must have a servant's heart and church leaders who are unwilling to serve are also unfit for their professional role. Through servant-hearted leadership, pastors exemplify the love of Jesus. In John thirteen, Jesus showed His disciples how to exercise servant leadership when He washed their feet. And, later in scripture, Paul observes that Jesus *"humbled himself and became obedient to the point of death—even death on a cross."* A new emerging model of pastoral leadership in these changing times is the servant leader. And, ministerial leaders would be well advised to practice the servant model in both their personal and professional lives.

While pastors must be servant leaders in these changing times, they should always practice one critical character trait in their personal daily lives: honesty. In his book *Character Is Destiny*, author, John McCain, (the Republican nominee for president in the 2008 general election) points out that honesty is a key ingredient in one's character. McCain, who was a prisoner of war during Vietnam, tells the story of Sir Thomas More.[5] More, who was a counselor to King Henry VIII, refused to sign an oath recognizing Anne Boleyn as the rightful queen. More knew that the oath denied the Roman Catholic Pope's authority over the Church of England, and in good conscience he could not sign it. Maintaining honesty and integrity to the end, More was ultimately killed by the king for his act of defiance. But, More's legacy is one of honesty and pure character in the face of tyranny. In short, as pastoral leaders, we have to do what is right in the eyes of God, not people. Some of the early disciples themselves were martyred because they would not compromise their faith in Jesus Christ.

In these changing times, people are looking for a faith that is real and uncompromising to the end. Pastoral leaders must maintain their honesty and integrity in all matters, including money and finances. In his book titled, *Your Money Counts*, author, Howard Dayton, points out that there are more than 2,350 verses about money.[6] Some pastors today have been accused of loving money to the point of compromising their honesty and integrity. But, 1 Timothy 6:10 says, *"For the love of money is a root of all kinds of evil, and in their eagerness to be rich some have wandered away from the faith and pierced themselves with many pains."* In my discussions with those who do not attend church, one of the most cited criticisms of church leaders is that we are more interested in money than people. In these changing times, we must put our focus on changed lives and the church's financial matters will take care of themselves. Furthermore, pastors must not accumulate debt and put their faith in material matters. In the Sermon on the Mountain, Jesus challenges us all with these words: *"Do not store up for yourselves treasures on earth, where moth and rust consume and where thieves break in and steal; but store up for yourselves treasures in heaven, where neither moth nor rust consumes and where thieves do not break in and steal. For where your treasure is, there your heart will be also."*

Aside from honesty and integrity in all personal matters, pastoral leaders must also honor their duty to be faithful parents who discipline their children. For those church leaders who have the privilege and duty of being parents, there is perhaps no greater job assignment on the planet. The Bible addresses the issue of raising responsible children. Proverbs 22:6 says: *"Train children in the right way, and when old, they will not stray."*
And, while Proverbs 22:6 targets all Godly parents, the letter of First Timothy especially addresses the parenting role of pastoral leaders. Paul advises bishops in 1 Timothy 3:4: *"He* [a bishop] *must manage his own household well, keeping his*

children submissive and respectful in every way." Furthermore, the apostle cautions deacons in 1 Timothy 3:12, "*...let them manage their children and their households well.*" In their book, *Parenting With Love and Logic*, authors, Cline and Fay, write the following wise words: "We (parents) are called to raise responsible children who make decisions, and live with the consequences of them."[7] Others are looking at church leaders to see how we are leading our homes. If we can't lead our homes, we certainly are not capable of leading an entire church!

Recently, my wife and I flew to Switzerland for a ten day visit. Meanwhile, we entrusted our seven-year-old son, Caleb, to his maternal grandparents. Unfortunately, while we were out of town, my mother-in-law was forced to check into the hospital. When we discovered that my wife's mother was not ill enough to dictate a flight back, our neighbors stepped up to the plate and cared for Caleb. He was with them for two days and nights. Upon returning, I spoke with my neighbors about our son's behavior. "He was absolutely perfect," our neighbor stated with a wide grin.

I couldn't help but feel a sense of pride and satisfaction as I listened to her comments. With his parents nearly 4,000 miles away, our son had been awesome. Maybe we need to take a vacation and fly away more often! But, truly it was a blessing to realize that seven years of Biblical training and discipline was bearing fruit in our son's life. As a pastoral leader, but perhaps even more so as a parent, I can attest that Biblical principles do work when raising children.

THE PASTOR'S PROFESSIONAL LIFE

The pastor's personal life certainly has an enormous impact

on his or her leadership. And, in turn, the pastor's professional leadership of a church has a tremendous impact on its effectiveness in ministry. A healthy long tenure of one lead pastor is key to growing a vibrant Biblical church.

In his book, *The Purpose Driven Church*, author and pastor, Rick Warren, makes the following assertion: "Healthy, large churches are led by pastors who have been there a long time....A long pastorate doesn't guarantee a church will grow, but changing pastors every few years guarantees a church won't grow."[8] Recently, when I was on staff at Riverside Park United Methodist Church in Jacksonville (where I served as the associate minister), I studied the history of pastoral transition there and noted that the church had twenty-four pastors in the last 100 years. That's an average of just over four years per pastor. Imagine a car stopping every four miles on a trip that lasts for one hundred miles. That is a lot of stops! Inevitably, with each pastoral leadership change, a church will head in a new or slightly different direction. With such tumultuous leadership change, it is difficult for a church to maintain a consistent vision, mission, and set of core values. As a result, the church loses sight of its ultimate destination and wanders aimlessly towards an unknown location. Christ never intended that for the church. On the other hand, his last words in Matthew's Gospel are very clear and concise regarding the vision and mission of the local church: *"Go therefore and make disciples of all nations, baptizing them in the name of the Father and of Son and of the Holy Spirit"* (Matthew 28:19). Therefore, healthy churches and denominations in these changing times must find a way to make sure that healthy consistent leadership of local churches is being realized.

In fact, Rick Warren compares pastoral changes at churches to a family getting a new father. Imagine if a child grows to the age of eighteen and has four different fathers. How will she turn out? Likewise, churches that have many pastoral changes will ultimately find themselves without a strong sense of vision, mission and core values. It is that simple!

In addition to a long tenure by one lead minister, local churches also need pastors who are committed to improving their leadership abilities. In his groundbreaking book, *The 21 Irrefutable Laws of Leadership*, John Maxwell writes that "Leadership develops daily, not in a day."[9] Maxwell, an ordained Wesleyan pastor, observes that it is absolutely critical for pastors to consistently hone their leadership skills. He argues that church pastors can increase their leadership abilities. In fact, he is so sold out on the topic of leadership that he says, "Whatever you will accomplish is restricted by your ability to lead others."[10] Referring to what he calls the "leadership lid," Maxwell believes that a pastor's leadership ability either binds or unleashes the gifts and actions of others. In other words, if a pastor has limited leadership capability then a "lid" is put over the church's ability to move forward in ministry. However, if the pastor's leadership capability is high, then the "lid" is off and the church can move ahead.

Healthy churches are led by healthy pastors who raise their leadership lids and allow the Holy Spirit driven power of the church to be unleashed. Unfortunately, too many churches are led by pastors who have a limited leadership ability. Such pastors are either lazy on the one hand or try to micromanage and dictate every decision and action of the church on the other hand. Other pastors, those with a "Messiah" complex, try to do everything themselves and end up being worn out.

A good Biblical illustration of empowering leadership is found in Exodus. In the eighteenth chapter of Exodus, Moses is beginning to feel overwhelmed by his role as judge over the people. Many are coming to him to dispute their cases against one another. So, his father-in-law, Jethro, advises him to select and train wise men to decide the smaller court cases. In turn, that allows Moses adequate time to judge the really serious ones. The plan is a hit and Moses follows through on Jethro's wise counsel. Likewise, pastoral leaders today need the wise counsel of men and women who are trained to raise our leadership lids. For instance, in my own professional life, I spend one weekend per year attending the Willow Creek Leadership Summit in our local area. And, in addition to that, I have completed courses and read many books with strategies about raising my leadership quotient. Nothing may be more critical in the church's life than a strong and competent leader who is led by the power of the Holy Spirit.

Another key leadership skill for pastors in the local church is practicing what Maxwell calls the "law of navigation." This leadership expert observes, "Anyone can steer the ship, but it takes a leader to chart the course."[11] A pastor's sense of vision for the church must be cast on a continual basis to remind the followers where the church is heading. Sometimes, stronger personalities in the church like to tell the pastor what to do, as if he or she is a "hireling," or an employee of the church. However, after forming a vision with the church's team members, it is up to the pastor to chart the course that will help the congregation reach its destination.

Several years ago, I was in a seminar where a new church pastor was recalling a heated conversation with a church member who would not back down on a plan to influence the church's destination. Finally, the exasperated pastor told him, "If you want a church, then drop everything you are doing, go to seminary and get your own church." As a result, the church member left the congregation, but the church continued to thrive and grow because it had charted a different course than the irate member had suggested. Sometimes, people mean well, (and sometimes not) but the pastor has been ordained with the authority and power to chart the course for the church's team leaders.

Though a leader may chart the course for a church, he or she does not go it alone. Rather, pastors are called to work with a team of individuals who help multiply his or her ability to lead. John Maxwell writes that "A leader's potential is determined by those closest to him."[12] In other words, a leader should be surrounded by a strong team of individuals who raise the leadership ability of the entire organization. For example, Jesus had the twelve disciples. Though different with respect to occupation and personality, these twelve apostles transformed the world for their Master.

With respect to church staff, Maxwell advises getting rid of the bad ones and keeping the good ones. However, he also counsels trying to raise up individuals within the organization to lead whenever possible. For pastors, that means making tough decisions which will influence and direct the church's vision, mission, and core values. A pastor's team must be committed to the vision, mission, and core values of the organization.

While pastors are called to work with a team of individuals surrounding them, they also have other challenges. For instance, the fact that pastors don't clock in and out of their jobs makes time management a key issue in the church leader's life. In short, healthy pastors of healthy churches use their time well. In his book titled, *First Things First*, Stephen Covey divides personal and professional activities into four major quadrants.[13] Quadrant one represents "crises, pressing problems, and deadlines." Quadrant two is "preparation, planning, relationship building, empowerment, prevention, values clarification, and true re-creation." Quadrant three symbolizes "interruptions, some meetings, some phone calls, and many pressing matters." And, finally, quadrant four amounts to everything else: "busywork, trivia, time wasters, 'escape' activities, irrelevant mail and excessive television." In summary, Covey notes that leaders should spend most of their time in quadrant two. In general, pastoral ministry has two extreme options when it comes to time. One can goof off and work a minimal amount "just to get by." Or, one can really put in the hours and eventually "burn out." Either option represents poor stewardship of time on the pastor's part. Rather, along with Covey, I argue that a pastor should spend most of his or her time in quadrant two. As the church's leader, a pastor should be spending a great deal of time investing him or her self in the mission, vision, and core values of the organization. And, many pastors need to spend more time empowering others to do ministry rather than trying to accomplish it all him or her self. In fact, when church leaders spend time empowering others to do ministry, they are allowing others to utilize their spiritual gifts for ministry. In 1 Corinthians 12, Paul lists the various spiritual gifts in the church. If the pastoral leader thinks that he or she has all these gifts at once, then he or she is absolutely crazy. The reality, of course, is that we are all called to ministry and the empowerment aspect of a pastor's ministry will save him or her time in the long run. For example, training someone else to help with hospital visits or visitation to the homebound, will allow the pastor more time to clarify and live out the larger vision, mission and core values of the church.

Empowering others to perform the church's ministry takes humility, since the leader is not the center of attention. Rather, the focus must always remain on Jesus, Who gave us a servant paradigm for leadership. The prophet Isaiah pointed forward in time to the "suffering servant," Jesus.

Jesus washed His disciples' feet and admonished them that the greatest one must be the servant of all. Later, Paul writes that Jesus was an obedient servant by dying on the cross. Service is at the very heart of the gospel. And, furthermore, it must be at the heart of leadership. In his book, *Jesus on Leadership*, author, Gene Wilkes comments, "A servant leader serves the mission and leads by serving those on mission with him."[14] Wilkes' book reveals seven principles of servant leadership, but I was especially captured by three of his insights regarding Biblical servant leadership.

First, Wilkes points out that servant leaders must be humble. For instance, in Luke 14:7-11, the parable reminds disciples to humble themselves and wait for God to exalt them. Timing can be critical in pastoral leadership. At times, leaders and churches might be willing to begin a ministry but it is not in "God's timing." Therefore, pastors and leadership teams must wait on the guidance of the Holy Spirit. God will exalt both us and the ministries we sponsor when the time is right.

Second, Gene Wilkes advocates that pastoral leaders should follow Jesus rather than seek a position. For example, in Mark 10:32-40, when James and John are seeking positions at the right and left hand of Jesus, the Lord responds that it is not His responsibility to assign them to those roles. Rather, James and John are to remain faithful followers. Too often, pastoral leaders may be tempted to "force" our way through ministry and not rely on the Holy Spirit to open doors for our ambitions. Our job is to remain faithful. Meanwhile, God's job is to open doors for His Spirit to guide and lead us as we go.

Finally, Wilkes argues that church leaders should find greatness in service. Mark 10:45 says, *"For the Son of Man came not to be served but to serve, and to give his life as a ransom for many."* Perhaps, the preeminent example of finding greatness in service is Mother Teresa. Until her death in 1997, she served faithfully among the poor in India, and was even a Nobel Peace Prize winner. She found greatness in her service to others through Jesus Christ.

Even as pastoral leaders work at being servant minded, professional ministry certainly can be a mental battleground. Ministry challenges not only our bodies and spirits, but also our minds. Notice that Jesus challenges his disciples to love God with all their heart, soul and *mind*. The evil one loves to infiltrate our thoughts and influence our actions. Therefore, healthy pastoral leaders must keep their minds strong in the Lord.

Several years ago, when I was suffering from mild depression and going through some stressful times, I picked up a copy of a book called, *Feeling Good*. In it, psychologist, David Burns, cites several mental errors that people make in their judgments. For example, some pastoral leaders may be good at "disqualifying the positive"[15] In other words, the evil one allows us to think that we are not making positive contributions to the church as pastoral leaders. Thus, we may be tempted to quit or "fish" for complements from those we serve. Another mental lapse that people suffer from involves "jumping to conclusions."[16] That is, we may assume something that is simply not true. Unfortunately, in pastoral leadership, some are tempted to jump to conclusions on a regular basis. As a result, communication can break down and a pastor's relationships can be adversely affected. Therefore, church leaders must learn to be patient and gather all the facts before responding to others, especially with regards to sensitive situations.

Another typical psychological error that people make is called "magnification" or "minimization."[17] In magnification, we tend to make a problem bigger than it is; in minimization, we tend to minimize the damage or danger of something. Both have severe consequences. For pastoral leaders, magnification may cause us to make a problem larger than it is, while minimization may lead us into minimizing the impact of an action or event. Again, ministry can be a battlefield of the mind and healthy pastors would be wise to heed these psychological cautions as he or she engages life in the church and community.

Aside from mental and psychological concerns, a final aspect of the minister's professional life that I will undertake here is the issue of multiplication in leadership. In other words, a healthy leader is committed to multiplying his or her leadership in the church. Just as Jesus identified, nurtured and equipped the first disciples, so we are called to do the same with the followers that God has entrusted to us. In his book, *Developing the Leaders Around You*, author, John Maxwell, challenges leaders of organizations to identify potential leaders, nurture them, and equip them for the mission. As one identifies potential leaders, Maxwell advises that they should be "people of character… influence… positive attitude…have effective communication skills… have a proven track record and be discontent with the status quo."[18] He further notes under the issue of character that a potential leader must "take responsibility, keep promises and meet deadlines."[19] Of course, the purpose of identifying potential leaders is to multiply the leader's effectiveness in the organization. No leader can be in all places at all times. Thus, leaders must train up others to do the work of ministry as they have been gifted. A minister who identifies, nurtures, and equips a visitation team is much more valuable to the church than a minister who simply visits alone. Note in Jesus' ministry that He identifies His first disciples by the lakeside in Galilee. Peter and Andrew, who had a fishing business were patient risk-takers who dedicated their lives to the profession. Thus, they made great candidates for disciples!

After identifying potential leaders, pastoral leaders must next nurture those under their care. John Maxwell counsels leaders of organizations to "believe in them, encourage them, share with them, and trust them."[20] Leadership is both a journey and a destination. As we nurture potential leaders, pastors are called to let those we identify know that we believe in their abilities. Furthermore, we should encourage them during times of disappointment and challenge. It is important to let potential leaders know that it is the response to disappointment rather than the event itself that marks a true disciple of Jesus. Next, we are also called to confide in and share with those we are nurturing for leadership. Mutual sharing and confidence reveal that we are humble, vulnerable, and willing to dialogue with them during the journey of leadership training. Finally, we are also called to trust potential leaders. We must allow them the opportunity to fail or they will never learn how to succeed. Failures must be seen as opportunities in disguise.

Ultimately, after we have identified and nurtured potential leaders, we must equip them for ministry. According to Maxwell, mentoring is a three step process consisting of modeling, mentoring, and empowering.[21]

In other words, show them how to do it, assist them as they do it, and then watch and encourage them as they do it themselves. In Jesus' own ministry, He showed and demonstrated God's healing powers. Then, He sent the seventy out to heal and teach. Afterwards, they came back and reported their progress to Him. No doubt, Jesus helped them hone their teaching and healing skills at this point in their ministry. However, He finally equipped them so well that they did the healing themselves. The Book of Acts is a living reminder of the healing and teaching powers of these first disciples.

They were so equipped to do ministry that it took place even in Jesus' absence after the resurrection. Now, that is a testament to the power of identifying, nurturing and equipping potential leaders!

SUMMARY

Pastoral leadership is a key ingredient in the recipe for a healthy church. And, healthy churches need healthy leaders who have healthy personal and professional lives. A pastor's personal life must be founded on an authentic relationship with Jesus Christ. Without that, nothing else in the leader's life even makes sense. Upon that spiritual foundation, pastoral leaders must be careful to observe moral boundaries, especially sexual ones, in their personal lives. If the pastor is single, then he or she is called to remain celibate. If the pastor is married, then he or she must remain faithful to the marriage covenant. Next, pastors must have healthy friendships. Leadership can be lonely; so, pastors must develop and maintain healthy relationships that express a genuine love for God and neighbor. In addition, pastors must also have a servant's heart and display that in the local community. Moreover, in the pastor's personal family life, he or she must be a responsible parent by following the guidelines in scripture for mothers and fathers.

The second major section of the chapter explored the pastor's professional life. Studies prove that healthy churches are led by lead pastors who hold a long tenure in the local church. Changing pastors every few years is a sure sign that a church will not experience vibrant growth.

Second, pastoral leaders cannot remain static. Rather, pastoral leaders must commit to continuously improving their leadership abilities in these changing times. Leadership is also a good topic of study for leaders these days. John Maxwell, a leading leadership expert, cites such leadership laws as the "law of the lid," the "law of navigation," and the "law of the inner circle." The "law of the lid" reminds us that an organization will never rise above the leadership capability of the leader. And, the "law of navigation" reminds us that a leader's job is to chart the course of the organization. Furthermore, the "law of the inner circle" is evidence that it takes a team of leaders to effectively lead an organization in the twenty-first century. Gone are the days of the lone ranger leader. Team leadership is the norm in a new era. Well-rounded leaders in these changing times will also be servant-leaders who embrace the model of Jesus as the "suffering servant." Leaders nowadays are advised that they must practice sound thinking, as well. Mental lapses like disqualifying the positive, jumping to conclusions, and magnification and minimization are tools of the enemy and may compromise our ability to lead effectively and successfully.

And, finally, a pastoral leader's professional life must include identifying, nurturing, and equipping potential leaders. Leaders come and go. They are born and they die. Thus, we must identify, nurture, and equip a younger generation of leaders who will lead churches in the twenty-first century.

Chapter 3

THE CHURCH'S WORSHIP LIFE

Healthy pastoral leadership is critical to building a healthy church in these changing times, and, nowhere is the pastor's leadership more needed than in the church's worship life. At a former church, we did a church and community survey in two local parks. Some of the people who took our survey pointed out that the purpose of the church was to worship. Indeed, some who responded to the survey questions felt that the most important mission of a church was to worship God in truth and spirit.

Healthy worship should certainly be the defining characteristic of Biblically based church. I will look at ten aspects of healthy worship here in chapter two:

- worshipping with God as the central focus
- Biblically based worship
- culturally relevant worship
- planning worship with excellence in mind

-authentic worship
-thoughtful mind-engaging worship
-practical worship
-the use of technology in worship
-experienced based worship (including the arts and drama)
-the importance of the sacraments in worship

WORSHIPPING WITH GOD AS THE CENTRAL FOCUS

One of my favorite books on how to do church in these changing times is Rick Warren's, *The Purpose Driven Church*. Regarding worship, Warren observes, "In genuine worship, God's presence is felt, God's pardon is offered, God's purposes are revealed, and God's power is displayed."[1] In short, worship should be all about God, not us. Today's American culture idolizes self-pleasure; however, worship always has and always should be about God's pleasure. Worship is about the creation worshipping the Creator. Worship is not about a church building. On the other hand, worship is about people surrendering their hearts to the living God. Worship is about the unholy sinner acknowledging his or her sin before a holy God. Worship must place God at the very center of its focus.

In our culture today, people are often tempted to put the pastor at the center of worship. And, at times, pastors, seeking an ego fix and power, have put themselves as the worship focus. But the heart of worship must be about Jesus or it simply becomes another form of idolatry. Just recently, I spoke with a congregation member who was upset with her pastor for a variety of reasons. Although she was well meaning, she made a remark that led me to believe that the pastor was the reason why she was attending a certain church. So, when that pastor did not meet her expectations, she was ready to move to another congregation. However, pastoral leaders would be well advised to remind people that God, not clergy, should be the centerpiece of worship. In some sense, modern contemporary worship service settings have reinforced the view that the pastoral leader should be the focus of worship. In some worship centers there is no cross and the focus falls entirely upon the one giving the message that day. Such an arrangement highlights the preacher rather than the One Who is being preached about—Jesus. Pastors and those they serve must find creative and consistent ways of reminding themselves that God, not the preacher, should be the sole focus in worship.

Another major issue present in both ancient and contemporary worship that distracts from worshipping God is physical location. That is, some people tend to be more concerned about where they worship rather than Who they worship. Once again, healthy churches in these changing times must always remain concerned about Whom we worship rather than where we worship. Too often, the church building becomes the focal point of worship to the detriment of our Lord and Savior Jesus Christ. In Jesus' day, the Jews and Samaritans had a major disagreement about where to worship. When Jesus confronted the Samaritan woman at the well in John 4:1-42, He points out that it is the spirit of worship, rather than the location of it, that really counts: *"But the hour is coming, and is now here, when the true worshipers will worship the Father in spirit and truth, for the Father seeks such as these to worship him. God is spirit, and those who worship him must worship in spirit and truth"* (John 4:23-24). Of course, soon after the resurrection of Jesus, early Christians worshipped in homes. And, nowadays, modern contemporary services are sometimes held in schools, movie theaters, restaurants, bars, outdoors, and in nearly every other venue imaginable. These different venues for worship outside the church walls are a good reminder that real worship is to be done in spirit and truth. Indeed, some worshippers get so attached to the "church building" that it becomes an idol. Such ones need to be reminded that true worship is that which honors the Lord Jesus Christ by putting Him at the center of one's attention.

BIBLICALLY-BASED WORSHIP

In addition to God being the center of all worship activity, it is also important to note that the Bible, God's Word, should be the foundation of a healthy worship service. In other words, the message, music and rituals of the worship service should always have the Bible as its source of inspiration. In one of the earliest descriptions of Christian worship, Luke the evangelist writes: *"They* [the earliest followers of Christ] *devoted themselves to the apostle's teaching and fellowship, to the breaking of bread and the prayers."* The format in Acts 2:42 is the most ancient "church bulletin" so to speak. This one verse in Acts incorporates the key aspects of a healthy worship service: preaching and teaching (the apostle's teaching), fellowship, the breaking of bread (Holy Communion), and the prayers. Let's take a brief look at these four elements of worship, each in turn.

First, **preaching and teaching** are at the heart of worship. Biblically-based worship means that the proclamation of the Word (preaching) must be included as a part of any healthy worship service. Now, preaching can take many forms (including art and drama), but it typically includes scripture reading and pastoral commentary on the passage. However, I am amazed at the number of pastors nowadays who read a scripture and never again refer to it in their message. That is not Biblical preaching! Biblical preaching involves sharing the transforming Word of God with those present so that they see its relevance for their daily lives. Preaching that merely "tells stories" or ignores the daily scripture text is not Biblical. The Biblical story should be woven into the story of people's lives so that they see that the living Word of God has the power to change lives today.

In addition to preaching and teaching, a second critical component of Biblically-based worship in Acts 2:42 is **fellowship**. I will talk more about the topic of fellowship in a later chapter. However, a brief analysis of fellowship is warranted here. Fellowship in some churches is simply about eating and burping. But, Christian fellowship is about more than a covered dish meal. In Greek the word *koinonia* (fellowship) connotes the deep spiritual and emotional attachment that disciples have with one another through their relationship with the risen Christ. Fellowship is the glue that binds a church together and causes them to be passionately committed to loving one another as Christ first loved us. Compassionate Christian fellowship cares for the wounded, heals the brokenhearted and suffers with the one who is in pain. Fellowship builds up the believer when one cannot make it alone. And, Acts 2:42 says that it is an essential element of worship. So, when we care for a Christian companion, we are engaging in an act of worship. And, when we dialogue with our brothers and sisters in Christ, we are speaking with Christ

Himself.

Even as fellowship is vital to the worship life of a body of believers, many congregations also **"break bread"** on a regular basis. In Acts 2:42, "the breaking of bread" is a reference to the practice of Holy Communion. It appears from early Christian writings that the most ancient churches practiced communion on a weekly basis. Of course, the celebration of the Lord's Supper originates with such passages as 1 Corinthians 11:23-26 and the gospel stories recalling the last week of Jesus' life. In any event, it is obvious that the early church revered the practice of Holy Communion and closely observed it. While Roman Catholic churches have observed communion on a regular basis for many years, some Protestant congregations are just beginning to also celebrate it more frequently.

While I will say more about it later in this chapter, suffice it here to say that Holy Communion reminds us to "continually remember" the sacrifice that Christ made for us until we come again. However, it also calls us to be in love and charity with our neighbors so that it will not be celebrated in vain.

A final element of Biblically-based worship is **prayer**. Of course, prayer is a pious practice that is woven throughout the fabric of the entire Bible. No doubt, prayer moves God and God moves in prayer. There is perhaps no greater act of faith on the part of a disciple than to pray. Prayer demonstrates faith in a holy God to act on behalf of creation. Prayer is the eternal force of nature. It moves hearts and souls. It stirs passions beyond belief and reminds us to honor God first in our lives. Prayer involves both speaking and listening. In corporate worship, prayer is especially powerful, for Jesus says in Matthew 18:20

that where two or three are gathered together, the Lord Himself is there with them. So, prayer is a key ingredient in the life of Biblically-based worship.

CULTURALLY RELEVANT

Nowadays, in these changing times, in this changing culture, healthy worship has to be culturally relevant. While true worship must not be held hostage by the culture, it must befriend it or cease to be relevant to people's lives. In his book, **The Purpose Driven Church**, Rick Warren says that worship must both reach those seeking a relationship with Jesus as well as building those who already believe in Him as the way, the truth and the life.[2] The music and message of the service must speak to people who live in the real world. In eighteenth century England, songwriter, Charles Wesley, often set his Christian hymns to tunes from the pubs in London. And, his brother, John, often preached a word that transformed how people viewed their daily lives. In other words, their ministries were so culturally relevant that they set off a revival that swept their country in the 1700's. Pastoral leaders and churches today would be well advised to follow their example.

If worship in your church is not culturally relevant to younger believers and non-believers alike then they will eventually find another place to go. The music must powerfully stir their hearts and minds to reach God; and the message must make a difference in their lives. Different music reaches different generations. As such, pastoral leaders and churches must target their music to reach a certain generation. If your music is reaching boomers and your message is reaching the elderly, then you cannot expect to reach generation X and Y.

Furthermore, different messages also reach different generations. In my experience, older generations who are dedicated to a local church will tolerate even the worst of sermons. (I know because I preached quite a few of those in my first church.) However, younger generations are busy and they want a message to make a difference in how they live their daily lives. Younger generations are inundated with television, cell phones, iPods and other technological advancements. Their attention spans are short. A relevant message delivered by a pastor that utilizes technology and tantalizes their senses reaches their hearts. So, while the Word of God itself does not change, the means of delivering that Word today has changed. Building faith in the lives of younger generations means taking advantage of any means necessary to make God's Word culturally relevant today.

PLANNING WORSHIP WITH EXCELLENCE

I once had a discussion with a pastor who bragged, "Most of the time, I don't even know what I am going to preach on Sunday until at least Thursday or Friday night. Sometimes, it is even Saturday!" He spoke as if the Holy Spirit did not give him inspiration for a message until late in the week. Fortunately, if pastoral leaders pray and discern God's will for our messages, inspiration can come much sooner than that.

Some church leaders and clergy act as if planning worship in advance takes the Spirit out of the process. But, in actuality, nothing could be further from the truth. When we work on our worship plans in advance, we show that we honor God and want to do our best to accomplish His will through our services. Worship that is poorly planned and executed communicates that we do not care enough to give God our very best. Imagine if you were expecting a famous celebrity or the President of the United States to show up at your service. Would it look any different? Of course it would and it should!

Yet, every Sunday some churches give a lackluster effort in worship then complain that "God was not in the service today." Ultimately, of course, the people gathered will probably blame the pastoral leader for not allowing them to sense God's presence and power. Therefore, it is up to clergy to lead worship planning that honors God in a true and real way. After all, a believer's purpose is to worship God so we should do it full out.

So, how does one begin planning worship with excellence in mind? First and foremost, a clergy leader should begin by forming a team of people for worship planning. Such a group should consist of the following people: pastors, music leaders and band members, people with the spiritual gifts and abilities of making music, as well as any others who can help with message series or sermon planning. I would also encourage pastoral leaders to have people on their worship planning teams with technical and worship arts/drama abilities. In these changing times, we should communicate the gospel in as many ways as possible. Drama, video, music and creative arts are just a few of the tools that pastors can utilize to get the message of God's love and salvation across to others. Let's face it. One's audience has a wide variety of people participating in worship. While some people are more touched by a powerful sermon, others are reached by a moving song. And, even as one is stirred to action by a provocative play or drama, another is deeply moved by a well executed video. There are multiple ways nowadays to proclaim the gospel, and churches in these changing times had better use every means necessary to share the gospel. Now, that doesn't mean that your church does everything. After all, no church can be good at everything. However, if your church has people talented in the art of making videos, then do it. And, if your church has others gifted with musical abilities, then by all means allow them to shine. The point is, use a variety of ways to share the gospel but make sure that they are done well. If people understand that we are worshipping to honor God, then surely they'll understand that worship planning must be done with excellence.

Planning worship with excellence involves organizing with an aim towards the long and short term. Long-term worship planning may involve planning for an entire year or two in advance. For instance, church leaders should set aside a focused time once per year to plan for the upcoming one. Such long-term planning may take place in a retreat type setting or over a weekend when worship teams have some extended time together. Often, events are put on a calendar for the upcoming year and nothing from the previous year is evaluated and new worship strategies are not introduced. However, it is important to evaluate what has worked and what has not worked as a team plans for the upcoming year. Moreover, teams should also brainstorm for new ideas and consider other creative means of worship as they approach an upcoming year. All team members should covenant together to be open to each other's suggestions while also asking the Holy Spirit to lead them.

In addition to annual long-term planning, worship team members should also do consistent short-term planning on a regular basis. Depending upon the size of the church, teams should meet either weekly or monthly to discuss planning for upcoming services. Even if meeting weekly, worship teams should look forward into the near future to plan their activities. It is also a good idea to have a "secular" calendar available, as most are more in tune with that than the "sacred" one. So, in addition to celebrating regular sacred days on the liturgical calendar (such as Christmas, Easter and Pentecost), worship teams might also plan something extraordinary for special national holidays as July 4th or Veteran's Day. And, often, such events as Thanksgiving and New Year's are excellent opportunities to plan special services or ministries. Churches that limit themselves to only planning for sacred days are certainly not in tune with these changing times.

AUTHENTIC WORSHIP

While planning for worship is always a critical part of the church leadership's life, praising God should always be done *"in spirit and in truth."* In John 4:23-24, Jesus says, *"But the hour is coming, and is now here, when the true worshippers will worship the Father in spirit and truth, for the Father seeks such as these to worship him. God is spirit, and those who worship him must worship in spirit and truth."* In other words, worship should be done in an authentic and genuine way. Worship should be led by the Holy Spirit and be done with an aim towards the truthful core values of scripture. Worship that glorifies people or the preacher is not real worship. Rather, worship that truly puts Christ at the center and places His truth in people's hearts is authentic. In today's cultural trend towards contemporary worship, there is somewhat of a tendency in large churches for praise to be experienced as a "performance" or a concert. Such "superficial" worship is not the kind that

God honors. Even in the large church setting, while music and the message must be done with excellence, there still needs to be the spirit of truth guiding all elements of the service. Therefore, one important question for worship planning teams to consider is, "Does our service reflect the fact that we are called by scripture to worship God in spirit and in truth?" If the answer is yes, then the team is on track. If not, then the worship planning team must devise ways for their service to be scripturally grounded in the eternal truths of Christ.

THOUGHTFUL WORSHIP

In his book, *The Purpose Driven Church*, author, Rick Warren, challenges pastors and leaders to make sure that worship is done in a "thoughtful" manner. He points out that Jesus calls us to love God with all our minds. So, Warren writes that worship must challenge the mind, as well as the heart and soul.[3] One criticism that is sometimes leveled against the church is that we don't engage people's minds enough. In addition, some who do not attend church believe that Christians are blindly following Biblical truths that are not supported by science or academics. In order to address other's concerns and to be guided by Biblical truth, we are called to take a thoughtful approach to worship by challenging people's minds. Christian writers such as Josh McDowell and Lee Strobel have written some intellectually stimulating books that support the truths of scripture with scientific and academic viewpoints. At one church, I took a group of youth through a book titled, *The Case For Christ,* by Lee Strobel. In it, he argues for solid historical evidence that supports the claims and ministry of Jesus in the New Testament. Pastors and worship leaders should share such thoughts in their praise services to convince doubters that Jesus is truly the way and the life. People who hear these scriptural truths will be empowered to go from such worship services and share the good news with others who don't know Christ. Worship services are an excellent opportunity to share the mind-engaging truths of the gospel with others to equip them for Christ's work.

PRACTICAL WORSHIP

In addition to engaging the mind, worship should also have practical implications in the real world. Sometimes, I honestly wonder whether some pastors and church leaders work and live in a "bubble." Earthquakes may kill thousands of people in Asia, and church leaders show up on Sunday and only acknowledge the needs of the church and their immediate family.

One of the most cutting criticisms leveled against the church by those who don't attend is that Christians are not in touch with the "real" world. And, I will have to admit, I have been to many church services that never speak to the practical needs in my life. Again, worship is intended to praise God not people; but, a worship service that does not address the needs of individuals in some way is out of touch with reality. In the Gospels, Jesus was constantly focused on meeting people's needs during His ministry. One needed physical healing. Another desired forgiveness. Still another wondered about how to restore broken relationships with friends and family. Jesus relied on the transformative power of scripture and the Holy Spirit to meet those needs. And, in doing so, He also transformed the world.

One critical area to address on a practical level is preaching. Messages must reach the hearts of people and lift them up to God, giving them hope while also changing their lives. Even a brief look at some sermon titles in the newspaper, on websites, and on church signs may draw a yawn from the most devoted believer. Sermon titles such as "The Holy Spirit" and "The Love of God," while Biblically sound, do very little to address the needs of a hurting world. However, message titles such as "Realizing Your Dreams," "The Key to Powerful Prayer," and "The Keys to Successful Teamwork," may be both Biblical and peak the interest and curiosity of hearers. Contemporary churches such as North Point Community Church in Alpharetta, Georgia, and Willow Creek Church in Illinois are growing by leaps and bounds because they are faithful to the Biblical text while also addressing the practical needs of people. Church leaders would do well to follow their example of balancing a Biblical approach to ministry with a practical perspective.

Another important practical area to address in worship is missions and outreach. Too often, churches divorce their missions and outreach efforts from their worship settings. Church leaders would be wise to integrate their mission and outreach ministries into their worship life.

Several years ago, we held a "Mission Sunday" when I was on staff at a large church in northeast Georgia. The ministries that we supported in the local community were invited to set up in our fellowship hall to share what they were doing. Participating ministries sent spokespersons, a well done poster board outlining their efforts, as well as video and personal testimony of their outreach efforts. We canceled our Sunday morning classes and allowed people to walk by and visit the various ministry tables. The spokespersons at those tables were allowed to recruit volunteers and explain how the church had supported their ministries. The response was remarkable. People who had been in the church for years had no idea that we "sponsored" some of these local ministries both financially and with volunteers. Some of the local community spokespersons shared about their ministries in our worship service. The mission Sunday was a successful event that also reminded our people that the church is making a difference in the community on a continual basis. Often, churches are doing more in the community than they realize, but we do not "market" ourselves well because we want to be humble. However, we would be wise to remember the words of Jesus in Matthew 5:16: *"In the same way, let your light shine before others, so that they may see your good works and give glory to your Father in heaven."*

TECHNOLOGY AND WORSHIP

Now, more than ever, modern technology should be integrated into worship services. While some congregations are resistant to technology on theological or financial grounds, it can play a strategic role in modern day worship services. Younger generations who grow up with television, video, and the internet are drawn to technology in a profound way. Churches that take advantage of technological innovation are on the cutting edge of reaching the younger generation. And, some recent articles suggest that technological ministries are among those growing at the fastest rate. Let's face it, the Great Commission said nothing about how to accomplish it, Jesus simply says *"Go make disciples."* A vital part of the worship experience in today's changing world will involve technology.

Several years ago, when I was serving at that large church in northeast Georgia mentioned earlier, another pastor on our staff attended his grandchild's baptism at nearby North Point Community Church in Alpharetta, Georgia. Andy Stanley, son of the very well-known Rev. Charles Stanley, is the lead minister at this church in North Georgia. The minister on our staff remarked to us after visiting the church that it was one of the most powerful worship experiences of his life. Apparently, one of the most moving parts of the worship service was a video interview with his daughter and her husband. Our fellow staff minister remarked that tears were flowing down cheeks as people watched the testimony of those proud parents. The video interview spoke to the transforming power of the Spirit to change lives and to their undying devotion and love for their child.

Of course, there are many other ways for churches to embrace technology: through video clips, music videos and presentations, and even taped drama or skit presentations. To embrace the future of changing lives in these changing times, churches must learn to envision the wonderful power of technology.

EXPERIENCE-BASED WORSHIP

The use of technology in worship is a subset of something larger that author, Craig Miller, refers to as "experienced-based worship." In these changing times, Miller observes, "What attracts the interactive/matrix thinking/iconic/culture-surfer is an experience that causes him or her to dig deeper to the truth."[4] So, while technology is simply one way to help people "experience" worship, the entire service itself should be experiential in nature. Just as people buy an experience when they have coffee at Starbucks or take a trip to Disney, so some in the younger generation are seeking an experience-based worship experience that draws them closer to God. The proclamation of the Word in an experiential service can be done via arts, drama, storytelling or media. And, the music should be an "indigenous" kind that "comes from the people and speaks to them in a form that they already understand."[5] For example, I grew up in the seventies and eighties when Rock-and-Roll was extremely popular. Currently, my favorite Christian band is Third Day. Their music speaks to me in a medium that I can understand while also connecting me to God. And, I have also discovered that the words of the band's music is so powerful that I find myself humming and singing their tunes to myself. Nowadays, music is an especially powerful way to reach the younger generation. Younger people are constantly inundated with sound as they listen to their iPods or drive their cars. Some churches are even giving away CD's to guests so that the powerful message of Christ reaches people in their homes and cars. Therefore, worship becomes more like a lifestyle, rather than a service that one attends once per week.

COMMUNION AND BAPTISM

One transformative way for participants to engage in experienced-based worship is through the two sacraments of Holy Communion and baptism. As mentioned earlier, Acts 2:42 lists the "breaking of bread" (Holy Communion) as a practice that the early disciples devoted themselves to on a regular basis. For worship to be healthy in these changing times, churches would be well advised to honor the practice of Holy

Communion on a regular schedule. Communion is a continual reminder of Christ's once and for all sacrifice for us. Furthermore, it also points to the future coming and reign of Christ. Sometimes, in churches that I have attended, the Holy Communion liturgy is read with no feeling or passion. Therefore, pastors and church leaders need to find ways to express the convictions behind this important rite in the church's life. A dramatic re-enactment of the communion liturgy or a passionate reading of it will reach hearers better than just a "dry" rendering of this important sacrament. I once experienced a mime communion at a youth retreat. It was one of the most powerful experiences of my life! In addition, churches might consider ways to practice communion on a more frequent basis. Often, a gradual introduction of the communion practice on a more frequent basis, along with some general education makes a more receptive environment for those who participate in the church's life. So, for example, if a church only celebrates communion on a quarterly basis, it may consider doing it once per month. And, for the church that only holds communion once per month, it may decide to do it on a weekly basis. However, the rite of communion should always be done with reverence and discretion that befits the Lord's Table.

In addition to Holy Communion, healthy churches also practice baptism in their worship services. Of course, baptism is a powerful event that transforms the lives of ordinary believers. Baptism reminds us that we die to sin and are raised with Christ forever. Healthy churches are those that baptize and receive new converts on a regular basis. In reality, like a plant growing in your back yard, a church either grows or dies. There is no in between! Churches that are baptizing people are churches that are moving forward in their ministries to reach the lost for Jesus Christ. Some churches have removed baptism to "separate services" attended only by immediate family members. Unfortunately, such a practice diminishes the role of the larger church to care for those who are baptized and it also takes away from the celebrative and experienced-based nature of praise and worship services.

Even if for practical reasons or emergency purposes someone has to be baptized outside the context of worship, churches would be well advised to tape those services and share them with the greater congregation. In addition, follow up needs to be done with those who are baptized so that they can connect to a small group where they might grow in their new found faith.

SUMMARY

Worship is an integral element of church life. After all, we were created for worship and when we cease to worship, we have ignored our purpose. Thus, healthy churches that practice Biblical worship will keep God the Father and Jesus Christ at the very center of worship life. If worship becomes all about the preacher or the people worshipping, then it is false and an abomination in God's sight. Furthermore, in these changing times that we live in, worship must be culturally relevant. The music and the message must speak to the daily lives of those who worship.

In his outstanding book titled, *Imagining A Sermon*, author and professor, Thomas Troeger, writes that clergy must use their imaginations to convey the message. Indeed, he observes,

"We trust, as did the biblical writers, that common things may be the source of revelation."[6] In other words, pastors must devise modern day parables that speak to the life-transforming power of the Holy Spirit. So, as leadership teams plan for worship, they must do so with excellence, recognizing that all that is done in the service must glorify Jesus. A regular meeting time and an extended time apart gives worship teams the healthy perspective they need to prepare worship with an aim towards excellence. Worship that is authentic, mind-engaging, and practical will reach those who worship at deeper levels than services that are superficial, mind-numbing, and irrelevant. And, in these changing times, where we are immersed with technology, churches and pastors must learn to utilize this contemporary resource in both creative and innovative ways. Technology especially reaches younger generations who are constantly bombarded with it in their daily lives. Craig Miller, a pastor and author, advocates that healthy churches also seek an "experience-based worship" style that resonates with those in the younger generation. He observes that people going to churches are looking for an experience rather than merely attending another church service. And, finally, the sacraments of Holy Communion and Baptism must be embraced in healthy worship settings. These ancient rites of the church must be given fresh life so that they are vital components of the gathered community as it moves forward into the twenty-first century in the name of Jesus.

Chapter 4

SMALL GROUPS AND DISCIPLESHIP

Imagine for a moment that Jesus had only spoken to large crowds and never developed disciple-leaders within a small group setting. If that had been the case, it is likely that you would not even recognize His name today. For those of us who have a personal relationship with Jesus, it is a frightening prospect to imagine life without Him. Fortunately, in the Gospels, it is very evident that Jesus spent a great deal of time teaching, mentoring, and building leaders within the small group setting. During His own lifetime, Jesus even released these disciple-leaders into ministry. In Luke nine, the evangelist reports the following:

"Then Jesus called the twelve together and gave them power and authority over all demons and to cure diseases, and he sent them out to proclaim the kingdom of God and to heal. He said to them, 'Take nothing for your journey, no staff, nor bag, nor bread, nor money—not even an extra tunic. Whatever house you enter, stay there and leave from there. Where ever they do not welcome

you, as you are leaving that town shake the dust off your feet as a testimony against them.' They departed and went through the villages, bringing the good news and curing diseases everywhere" (Luke 9:1-6).

In the Gospel passage above, Jesus affirms the concept of discipleship by doing the following: (1) He forms and teaches a group of twelve, (2) He gives them power and authority, (3) He sends them out to do ministry and instructs them as to how to carry it out, (4) He tells them to leave the results to God and (5) they follow through on His explicit instructions. In short, then, Jesus models discipleship for the twelve and builds that leadership group into a team that will transform the world. Jesus, Himself, is the ultimate disciple-leader, as He demonstrates time and time again.

In chapter four, we will take a look at a healthy small group structure, talk about developing the leadership within it, outline the importance of and discuss strategies for birthing new groups, and examine the importance of targeting when forming small groups. Small groups are like the root of a plant. If the root becomes diseased and rotten, then the entire plant will die. And, so it is with small groups. If small groups begin dying within the church, then eventually the larger church will hemorrhage and die unless radical surgery is performed. If people are simply attending worship services, but not active in small groups, then their faith will remain at an immature level, like new fruit on a tree. So, let's turn now and look at how to keep small groups healthy so that the church will thrive in these changing times.

SMALL GROUP STRUCTURES: REACHING AND RECEIVING NEW MEMBERS

In his book, *NextChurch.Now*, Craig Miller closely examines the structures of small groups and makes some insightful recommendations.

In addition to his perspective, I will share my own thoughts in the section before you concerning how to put together a healthy small group. According to Miller, the first step for building a small group is to reach and receive new members.[1] Of course, when forming a small group from scratch, church leaders will want to develop a core group of individuals to launch it. Within that core group, I have found it helpful to have at least two key leaders who play the lead role in organizing and building up the small group.

When Jesus sent out the seventy to do mission in Luke 10:1-12, they went in pairs. I believe that Jesus sent them out in pairs for several reasons. First, Jesus did so for safety purposes. The highways and byways could be dangerous places for robbers and bandits were very active in that day and Jesus wanted the disciples to return safely. Second, Jesus wanted the pair to support each other during difficult times. Sharing the gospel is no easy task. It requires a lot of mental strength and when one disciple got discouraged the other would be right there to encourage him. Finally, I am hypothesizing, but I believe that Jesus sent the disciples in pairs with complimentary spiritual gift sets so that maximum ministry could occur. As small group leaders in today's world, we would do wise to follow the example of Jesus. Small groups that engage in evangelism and missions should always practice good safety measures. Keeping people safe at church and in the community should be an important priority for modern day congregations. People are looking for a safe place to live out their God-given purpose, as well as a place where their children can do so in safety. In addition, co-small group leaders can support each other during trying times. Ministry is a challenging task and leaders always feel more confident when a co-leader or assistant is appointed to help them. With people's schedules nowadays, it is important to have a second person, due to vacations and job responsibilities. I have often found that people are more willing to volunteer as small group leaders if they have someone to assist them with leading the group. And, finally, small group leaders should be appointed that have complimentary gift sets. If two co-small group leaders have the same spiritual gifts, then they might be too alike to offer a balanced perspective. Differing points of view can often be a good thing when it comes to co-leading a group because such a style honors the varying perspectives of its members. But, in any case, small group leadership should always focus on reaching out and receiving others into one's fold. Otherwise, the small group may become so inward focused and static that it ceases to be an instrument of life transformation and change within the church.

Within the small group setting, reaching out and receiving others often happens one person or couple at a time. I have often found that a personal invitation is the best way to invite and receive new members into one's small group. Even in the age of email and cell phones, sometimes a face to face conversation is still the most effective way to involve someone in a small group. Within your small group, there should be someone designated for hospitality who is committed to inviting and developing relationships with potential new members on a continual basis.

General announcements such as, "We should all invite someone next week," do very little good in today's modern communication world. A specific person who is specifically trained and/or equipped for the mission of hospitality can help transform and renew the small group as some people inevitably leave due to job changes, moves, etc.

SMALL GROUP STRUCTURES: CONNECTING TO GOD THROUGH WORSHIP/ DISCIPLESHIP

In addition to reaching and receiving new members through invitational hospitality and evangelism, small groups must keep and build its members individually through worship and discipleship.[2] Recently, I had a conversation with a friend who was giving serious consideration to leaving a church. She is a person who is very mature in her faith and has a lot to offer any church fortunate enough to have her walk through its doors. When I asked her why she was thinking about leaving, she told me that the church offered no small groups that were really serious about delving deep into the scriptures. Unfortunately, her perspective is shared by others who struggle to find a church that is really serious about doing an in-depth Bible study. Too often, small groups become nothing more than social clubs that are devoted simply to "being with each other" or having a meal together. While fellowship is an important component of the small group structure that will be discussed later in the chapter, worship and discipleship should be paramount for their lives together. When possible, small groups may find it helpful to attend worship together. Small group leaders should note whether their members are attending worship services on a regular basis. Small group members who attend worship infrequently or not all should be encouraged to do so in obedience to God's Word (Hebrews 10:25).

Moreover, small groups should dig seriously into the Word of God as they seek to do life together. In my own experience leading and co-leading small groups, I have found it helpful to distinguish between "topical studies" and "Bible studies." That is, while some studies lend themselves to "topical" themes such as parenting or marriage, others are Bible study driven and simply dig deeply into the word on a regular basis. For pastoral and church leaders, perhaps the real issue is that any study be based on scripture. Some topical studies become so focused on parenting or marriage themes that they lose sight that the foundation of those studies must be God's Word. Of course, short-term parenting or marriage classes are fine to offer in the church's life. However, I am merely suggesting that the time set aside for serious small group study should involve digging deeper into scripture. In these changing times, healthy churches will offer up steak and potatoes in their small group settings rather than yogurt and cottage cheese. Let's face it.

People are hungry for the Word of God in this time of spiritual famine. Therefore, churches must prepare their troops for the spiritual battle that is ahead of them as they face their daily lives.

SMALL GROUP STRUCTURES: NURTURING AND STRENGTHENING

Even as healthy small groups seek to connect their members

to God through worship and discipleship, leaders should also help connect them to each other by nurturing and strengthening their personal relationships.[3]

In other words, Christian fellowship is an important component of small group life which should not be ignored by pastors and church leaders. In a sense, fellowship is the "glue" or "mortar" that holds the small group relationships together. 1 Peter 5:6-7 says, *"Humble yourselves therefore under the mighty hand of God, so that he may exalt you in due time. Cast all your anxiety on him, because he cares for you."* It is humbling to be part of a small group. We can cast our anxieties on the Lord in each other's presence, lift up our most intimate prayer concerns and care for each other and the community at large all at the same time. Small group fellowship often means allowing ourselves to be subject to the will of God through the Holy Spirit's moving within the group itself. And, perhaps, it is most humbling when small groups take care of each other and people within the group find themselves as recipients of member care.

Several months ago, I received word from someone in our church that a young man had been in a serious car accident. His mother was a member of our church and was very involved in one of our small groups. For one week, I visited the young man and his family in the intensive care unit of a nearby hospital. At the end of that week, the young man died. It was a tragic situation and the mother asked me to perform the young man's funeral. The day was beautiful and the sun was shining brightly through the branches of the large tree adjacent to where the young man was to be buried. As people slowly made their way to the graveside, I sat by the bereaved mother, held her hand and spoke with her. I had my back to the place where most of the funeral guests were arriving. Finally, as I took my place and the service began, I looked up and saw most of the members of the woman's small group standing behind her as she grieved the tragic loss of her son. At that very moment, I was reminded about the power of small groups.

On most days, those of us in our small groups probably take them for granted. However, on that day the mother's small group took very good care of her. After the service, the small group organized some food from our church and took it to the woman's house. And, in the weeks since her son's death, she has received cards, phone calls and visits from members of our church, and especially her small group. Small groups are there to care for each other and they remind us of Christ's love. After all, He was the leader of the ultimate small group—the twelve disciples.

SMALL GROUP STRUCTURES: SENDING THEM TO LIVE AS CHRISTIAN DISCIPLES

Small group fellowship is an integral part of the small group structure, but, small group life doesn't end there. Most of us live in the real world and the ultimate test of small group life may be whether or not members are released into ministry and mission in the world. So, author and pastor, Craig Miller, insists that small groups must send members out into the real world to lives as Jesus' disciples.[4] In these changing times, small groups must be engaged in the struggles going on in their local and global communities. In Acts 1:8, Jesus says: *"But you will receive power when the Holy Spirit has come upon you; and you will be my witnesses in Jerusalem, in all Judea, and Samaria, and to the ends of the earth."* Interestingly, the verse here in

Acts makes a geographical movement from the local (Jerusalem) to the global (the ends of the earth). There is no coincidence, then, that Jesus is calling both the ancient disciples and believers today into ministry and mission both locally and globally. And, an added benefit is that when we go out into the world in ministry and mission, we also have the opportunity to share the good news of Jesus with others. Of course, that is an excellent time to receive and reach new people for our small groups, thereby completing the cycle of the small group structure. However, in any event, as we engage in ministry and mission in our local communities and abroad, people both within and outside the small group see that we are making a difference for Jesus Christ.

In these changing times, younger generations want to see the church doing something. They are more impressed by our actions than our words. Doing mission both here and overseas says that we are serious about our calling to be disciples for Jesus Christ. There are so many ways for small groups to become a vital part of their communities. For example, last fall, members of my small group spent one Saturday building a home for Habitat for Humanity in a poor area of our city. We all agreed that it felt good to be part of something larger than ourselves in the name of Jesus.

DEVELOPING LEADERSHIP WITHIN THE SMALL GROUP

In his book, *Developing the Leaders Around You*, author and leadership expert, John Maxwell, talks about the importance of modeling, mentoring, and empowering leaders.[5] In modeling, we demonstrate the behaviors that we want mimicked. In mentoring, we advise someone else on how to carry out a task. And, in empowering, we equip and allow someone else the freedom to do something on his or her own.

In my own experience as a small group participant and leader, this is the number one area where many small groups falter. Without the right leadership, a group will die on the vine. Indeed, leadership can and will make or break a group. Most small groups would do well to develop and equip people in the following areas of leadership:

1. Teaching – at least two people should be developed in the area of teaching. Preferably, these people should have some gifts and abilities in this area, or people will eventually quit attending the small group. Good solid Biblical teaching is especially appreciated in today's modern church.

2. Hospitality/Member Care Host – at least one person should be skilled in the area of hospitality and membership care. Hospitality involves inviting new members to join the group, as well as making them feel welcome when they attend. And, as for member care, that involves contacting people in the small group when they do not attend or are sick or hospitalized. Again, membership care is critical and should be consistent from one person to another. For example, if one small group member gets no contact while in the hospital while another receives outstanding care, the group will perceive the inequity and the unity of the group will be compromised.

3. Fellowship Facilitator – Again, at least one person should serve as a fellowship facilitator for small group life. Ideas such as retreats, workshops, and simple social outings will help draw the group closer together. Groups that never really "bond" in the fellowship area have little chance of long term survival because members never really feel close to each other.

4. Ministry and Mission Manager – If a small group is to really thrive and be healthy, it must exist for something outside itself. A stream that does not flow anywhere else becomes a stagnant pool of algae. Jesus lived out His life in the real world. And, we do too. Ask yourself and your small group, "What are the needs right here in our local community?" And, ask yourselves, "How can we get involved right here in our area to help meet those needs?" Furthermore, you might ask yourselves to address global needs that affect the entire planet. Of course, your small group cannot meet every need in your local area or on the globe. So, make sure to find some common ground and target a specific need in your area. For example, you might decide to focus your efforts on helping children, the elderly, or the environment.

The bottom line is that it must be something that most people in your group feel passionate about. Otherwise, you will get half-hearted interest and results in your ministry and mission efforts.

HEALTHY SMALL GROUPS BIRTH NEW SMALL GROUPS

In the world of nature, something that is healthy gives birth to someone or something else that is healthy. For instance, a healthy plant may blossom and give birth to another plant when transplanted. And, in the life of the church, a healthy small group may grow large enough to birth another. If everything goes well, your small group will grow. As it grows and your numbers increase, at some point you might consider giving birth to another small group. Once a group gets so large that members no longer share an intimate knowledge of each other's faith journey, it may be time to begin a new group.

As a general rule, when most groups get in the 15-20 person range, it may be time to begin a new one. In my experience, I have found that it is best to focus on a specific demographic (if possible) when beginning a new group. For example, you might want to target parents raising young children or singles over the age of fifty, depending upon your setting. Often, people with very little in common make poor candidates for the same small group. It is not that these people might dislike each other, rather, it is that they are so different that there are few bridges for communication and fellowship to take place.

First, consider the core members of the new small group that is being birthed. Are they singles? Are they married? Are they young or old? Such issues really matter when putting together a new small group. Aside from demographic concerns, another possibility for forming a new group might be to base it on interests of potential members. Do the potential members prefer a "pure" Bible study or are they more attracted to topical studies such as parenting, the single life, or living as a married couple? Sometimes, the interests of the potential members might prevail over any demographic similarities among them. The bottom line is that the new group must covenant or agree on a foundation for their group or else it has very little chance of succeeding.

START NEW SMALL GROUPS ON A REGULAR BASIS

I discussed one model for birthing a small group above—the parent-child method. However, church leaders and pastors might also consider beginning a small group from scratch. Once again, a major issue from the beginning will be the core group of individuals who want to start a new group. In my experience, if there is not a committed core group of at least ten, it will be difficult to sustain a group over the long haul. (Or, you could just remain a very small group!) For one thing, in the twenty-four hour a day, seven days a week culture that we live in, it is challenging for people to be there for every meeting. And, it can become a numbers game of sorts. For instance, if you have fourteen young people in a small group, you can count on about half being there on any given Sunday (unless your members are unusually committed and live and work near their homes). At times, you will have more there and at other times you will have less. So, a healthy small group should begin on the basis of ten committed members who are sold out to God and each other.

When starting a new class from scratch, I also think it is a good idea to target it for demographics (i.e. parenting, marriage, singles, age groups) or interests for the reasons outlined earlier in this chapter. In my experience, a group that targets no one will reach no one. For instance, last year I began a small group after a short-term parenting class at our church. I wanted to target parents and do a series of studies with that particular demographic. However, I was advised by someone else "to open the group up to anyone who wanted to come." So, against my better pastoral leadership judgment, I did so. The result? The group disbanded several weeks ago. Our small group did not even make it one year. In my estimation, a major reason for failure over the long haul is that we did not target the class towards young parents.

Now, while we are in a smaller church setting with limited numbers, the truth of the matter is that if you target no one that is exactly what you will get…no one. Furthermore, during the months that we were together, I felt that the group never really bonded because the members sometimes had very little in common. Of course, I know that there can be exceptions to this general rule of targeting, but nowadays it is probably a strategy that would serve most church settings well. Unless small group members have been together for years and have an intimate knowledge of each other's lives, it is unlikely that they can bond unless they have some common ground.

When beginning a new class, it is also a good idea to consider inviting new people from outside the church. People in the community are more comfortable coming to a new small group than one that has been established for years. Long-running small groups are less likely to attract new people in the community than one in its infancy. The main reason for this is, since the group is in its infancy and non-church members are guests, they feel more comfortable in a setting where everyone else is also new. The old adage that "like attracts like" is especially true in small group life. Even a church that has been in existence for years should consider beginning new small groups on a regular basis. It not only gives non-members an entry point into the church, but also serves as a renewal movement within the larger congregation.

SMALL GROUP TOPICAL CLASS IDEA: MARRIAGE

Marriage is under attack in America. Different studies consistently show that about one half of all marriages end in divorce. Divorce always has tragic consequences within a family and can also lead to poverty, homelessness, and great emotional pain. And, of course, children are always impacted either directly or indirectly by a divorce in their families. So, most churches would be well advised to target at least one or more of their small group studies towards the issue of marriage enrichment (or offer it as a short term class). The Bible addresses the issue of marriage many times, including in the Gospels, First Corinthians chapter seven, and a few other New and Old Testament passages.

Recently, I also ran across another good book on the topic of marriage. The book is simply titled, *Marriage*, by Bill Hybels. In the book, he examines everything from finances to romance. In fact, he writes, "Couples who are unhappy with their marriages often admit that what disturbs them more than anything is the lack of romance."[6] Who knows? Discussing romance and a few of those steamy passages in Song of Songs might really get people to attend your new small group! But, in any event, churches, of all places, should be facilitators of marriage enrichment and help preserve the marital bond.

COVENANT: PRACTICING A BIBLICAL CONCEPT IN SMALL GROUP LIFE

One critical component of small group life is the notion of covenant. Whether written or spoken, covenant carries with it the idea that two or more parties are agreeing to terms and conditions that are important to all involved. In the book of Genesis, Abraham agrees to a covenant with God, the sign of which was circumcision. Thus, covenant is a Biblical concept and one that plays a very important role in the scriptures. Jesus, Himself, is even referred to as the "new covenant." So, how does the covenant idea apply to small groups and why is it important?

Covenants are important for small groups because they spell out the conditions under which life will be carried out together. When people enter into a relationship with a small group, they have certain preconceived notions about how life should happen within that group. A covenant that is developed and agreed to in a team format by the entire group constitutes the best arrangement possible for this concept to become a reality. The covenant will serve as the guideline for how the group relates to each other. Members who violate the covenant must be called into accountability by a group leader or forsake their place within the small group community.

Here is a sample small group covenant:

"The group members of the Faith Weavers Class pledge the following:

1. We pledge to be present at every meeting if at all possible.

2. We promise to prepare for every group meeting by reading assigned materials and/or otherwise preparing for our class experience.

3. We will respect each other by mutual sharing (so no one dominates the group), active listening, and participating in all group events with an open heart and mind.

4. We place our studies and our lives upon the foundation of God's Word so that it will serve as a lamp unto our feet and a light to our paths.

5. All studies and discussions will be relevant to our daily lives.

6. We pledge to serve in a specific role within the small group and not just be an attendee.

7. Furthermore, we promise to commit our group to five major purposes:

    • Worship: We want to be faithful to attend worship on a regular basis with other group members if possible.

    • Discipleship: Our group will be a place of serious study so that we can form ourselves in light of God's Word and example.

- Evangelism: We pledge to invite newcomers to our fellowship on a regular basis. We don't want to become a closed community.

- Fellowship: We will do at least one major fellowship event per month. We will open up our homes and our hearts to each other.

- Ministry and Missions: Our group will do one major ministry and mission event every quarter. In addition, we may choose to do some local and/or global ministry on an ongoing basis in obedience with Jesus' call to be in mission at both home and abroad (Acts 1:8).
(Note: The five purposes outlined above are adopted from Rick Warren's book, *The Purpose Driven Church*.)

If you or someone else you know is beginning a small group, I strongly urge you to consider drawing up a covenant such as the one above and have every member sign and agree to it. Along the way, as new members come and others go, you might consider changing your covenant somewhat to reflect the gifts and abilities of your new members. However, the covenant outlined above does give a basic overview of important ideas that would be helpful in most any covenant group. For example, if people are not present or prepared for group meetings, then there is little possibility that they can ever spiritually mature. Group leaders should boldly insist that a covenant be developed, adopted and signed by the group. Without an agreed upon destination, your group may be headed for nowhere.

SUMMARY

Small groups are absolutely critical to the life of a healthy church. As Jesus, Himself, showed, leaders can be mentored and matured in the small group setting. If Jesus had only preached to the crowds and never developed leaders within the context of a small group, then His legacy might have been lost. In his book, *NextChurch.Now*, author and pastor, Craig Miller, discusses the structure of healthy small group life: "reaching and receiving new members, connecting to God, nurturing and strengthening members and sending believers into the world to live as Christian disciples" are all important concepts that can transform lives for Jesus Christ.

Moreover, leaders must be developed within the context of small groups so that they will experience longevity. Small groups without good leaders are bound to fail in the long run. And, as small groups grow and become healthy, they should consider giving birth to other groups. Just as multiplication is the sign of a healthy church, it is also the sign of a healthy small group. Church leaders and pastors might also consider starting new groups from scratch. This approach involves identifying a core group, drawing up a covenant, and developing leadership as the group moves forward. One topical contemporary issue that some small groups may address is marriage. In our culture, the institution of marriage is under attack so church leaders and pastors would be wise to teach marriage enrichment as part of their ongoing education within the small group setting where appropriate. Finally, small groups should draft, adopt and sign a covenant as a sign of their commitment to God and to each other within church life. Small groups are certainly the engine which drives the church forward. The pastor or a designated church leader may even act as a "small groups coach" to carry out the ideas presented in this chapter. Coaching and mentoring your small group leaders is an important and necessary process for the long term health of the church. Without healthy small groups in these changing times, the church has little hope of constructing change either within or outside of the walls.

Chapter 5
EVANGELISM

Simply defined, evangelism means "good news." In Christian circles, evangelism connotes sharing the Good News of Jesus Christ with non-believers. In the American culture, I believe that we live in a time of "evangelism famine." While some inside the church are comfortable sharing the Good News of Christ with those overseas, we tend to overlook those who we come in contact with daily in our local neighborhoods. And, even as the church is growing in Asia and Africa, we are struggling to make headway in Europe and North America. In fact, some studies show that Christianity is declining in both Europe and North America. Evangelism is certainly hard work. It calls us out of cultural comfort zones and into the lives of others on behalf of Christ. But, the Bible challenges us as individuals and churches to do evangelism. Perhaps the most famous Biblical quote regarding evangelism is the Great Commission of Jesus: "*Go therefore and make disciples of all nations, baptizing them in the name of the Father, and of the Son and of the Holy Spirit*" (Matthew 28:19).

In this chapter, I will take a look at how the church can practice healthy evangelistic strategies in these changing times to fulfill the Great Commission. First, we will take a look at strategically focusing a church's evangelistic efforts. Along the way, we will discuss defining the target audience, doing demographic work, figuring out who the church can best reach, and exploring which styles of evangelism best fit your congregation. Second, we'll then turn to look at how churches can best equip their people to do personal evangelism. According to author and pastor, Scott Wilkins, ninety percent of the people who were baptized at North Point Community Church in the Atlanta area (where Andy Stanley is the lead pastor) were invited by someone else.[1]

No doubt, personal evangelism is perhaps the most important way that many people initially become connected to a church. So, pastors and church leaders would be well-advised to equip and encourage their members to do personal evangelism. In the third place, we'll look at how pastors and leaders can practice church-wide evangelism strategies that will help them reach their communities. Thus, while personal evangelism is important, a healthy church will also look at how large scale events can help reach others. And, finally, we will conclude the chapter by studying how practicing hospitality can invite and encourage non-believers to join the church fellowship. In these changing times, evangelism must be a top priority for believers and churches. Let's begin the journey to share the Good News.

TARGETING THE CHURCH'S EVANGELISTIC EFFORTS

As mentioned earlier in the work here, one of my favorite books on how to do church is Rick Warren's, *The Purpose Driven Church*. In this groundbreaking book and incredibly great read, Pastor Warren points out that churches must have a "target" for their evangelistic efforts. He writes, "No single church can possibly reach everyone. It takes all kinds of churches to reach all kinds of people."[2] I absolutely agree with Warren's assessment.

Growing up on a farm in North Carolina as a child, we often went fishing. If we wanted to go cat fishing in the river, we would take some chicken livers and fish on the bottom. If we wanted to fish for bass, we would get a plastic worm and hit the local pond. On warm summer evenings, we would toss out that plastic worm near the edges of the pond and giggle it on top of the water. Before you knew it, a bass would literally jump out of the water to grab that worm and the fun would begin. At other times, we would go dig up some earthworms and fish for bluegill. We would put a cork (float) on our line and watch as it bobbled on the water. And, when that float went under, we would set that hook and reel in bluegill that often weighed up to a pound. Simply put, we targeted our fishing efforts. Fishing for bluegill with a cork on the river would yield few results. The key was knowing what type of fish you were fishing for…only then could you decide what bait and fishing hole you would use.

A similar evangelistic strategy must exist for churches. Often, pastors and churches have no agreement or even an idea about who they are fishing for. Sometimes, the answer is, "whoever walks through the door." But, the reality is, most churches will reach a fairly homogenous group of people, unless that church has a very strong core value of multicultural ministry and is within that same community context. So, how should churches go about defining their targets?

Rick Warren suggests that churches must define their targets in four ways: geographically, demographically, culturally, and spiritually.[3] Simply put, defining the target geographically means to "identify where the people live that you want to reach."[4] Even though Warren suggests that most people are willing to drive up to fifteen or twenty minutes to attend church, there are exceptions. Due to relationships with others in a given church or the strong pull of a given church for any number of reasons, some people are willing to travel much further to attend. On the other hand, artificial barriers such as highways, construction detours, and other transportation issues make it difficult for some churches to reach those within a reasonable target area. In any event, the rule of thumb is that your church's leadership should establish a geographical target area within a given radius of your church location. Unless your church's ministry has a regional or national impact, it will probably be nearly impossible to have many devoted members who live more than thirty or so minutes from your church. Again, there are exceptions, but generally speaking the further people are away from your area, the less likely you are to reach large numbers of them.

During the summer of 2008, gas was nearly four dollars per gallon. With those prices, it is difficult for most people to justify driving a long distance from their homes to attend church services. As churches define their geographical target area, it would be helpful to have a local map handy to circle and designate exactly where that is. Everyone on your leadership team, and even those in your church, should have a good idea about where your target area is. That way, as you develop your evangelistic strategy, there will be no questions about the area that you are trying to reach.

Of course, in addition to geographic work, church leadership teams also must engage in demographic efforts to decide who they are going to reach. In most cases, author, Rick Warren, recommends that churches define their targets with respect to age, marital status, income, education, and occupation.[5] So, the church's leadership team must ask the question, "Who lives in our geographical target area?" If your church is located in a geographical target area that is dominated by people over fifty-five then that fact should certainly inform both your target and your evangelistic strategies.

Demographic questions such as the following are helpful to ask:

> "Are the people in our geographical target area single or married?"
>
> "Are the people in our geographical target area high, medium or low income?"
>
> "Are the people in our geographical target area high school or college graduates?"
>
> "Are the people in our geographical target area blue

collar or white collar workers?"

Such questions will allow you to discover your community and begin to develop your evangelistic strategies. Demographic information can be helpful because the community around your church is constantly in flux. Sometimes, church leadership assumes that most people in the community meet a certain demographic criteria when actually nothing could be further from the truth. For example, your church may be trying to reach young urban family professionals in a neighborhood that is dominated by older blue collar workers. If so, your efforts will probably not bear as much fruit as you think. While some demographics can be expensive to access, much local information is available at your public library. And, for those serving in denominational settings, your administrative offices typically have a ton of demographic tools available to you at reduced or no cost at all. If your church has not done demographic work in the last ten years, I think you would be well advised to get on the band wagon and do that as soon as possible. In these changing times, people often move and some communities change seemingly overnight. I believe that we have a Christ-given imperative to know who lives in our neighborhoods. After all, if we do not know who lives there, how can we possibly reach them with the good news of Jesus Christ?

In addition to researching and applying demographic data about their geographic target areas, churches should also study their contextual cultural milieu. Broadly defined, culture simply means "a way of life." Rick Warren writes that culture represents the "lifestyle and mindset of those who live around your church."[6] There are various tools and assessment techniques for figuring out the culture of one's community. First, you might read the local newspaper and follow current events in your community. Ask yourself, "What are people really passionate about in this area?" Perhaps, people are really concerned about the environment, crime, or even the lack of entertainment in the area. Local survey results and community trends are sometimes published in local papers. Such information can be an extremely valuable source of information about how to reach the community at its greatest point of need.

Second, a clever way to discover what is happening in one's community is to ask, "Where do people hang out around here?" Several years ago, when I was serving as a pastor in a small North Carolina town, I spent quite a bit of time at the local barber shop.

If you knew what I looked like at the time, you would laugh. Even at that young age, I had a classic male horse shoe pattern baldness thing going on and my hair rarely needed a cut. (It is even worse now!) So, why did I hang out in that smoke-filled barber shop so much? It was to discover the culture of that small town. I will have to say, I often learned more in a ten minute visit to that barber shop about the town than I did in a month of Sundays at our local church.

Currently, I live in Florida near the beach. If I want to know what is going on in the beach area, I show up around the pier or visit the local restaurants. In my immediate neighborhood, I often take a bike ride, go to a local park, or attend a little league game in my area. I learn a lot about the culture of our community in those settings—sometimes, even more than I really want to know! And, where do people congregate in your area? Unfortunately, some pastors and church leaders are so immersed in their church settings that they rarely venture out to discover what is really going on in their local communities.

A third way to unearth what is going on in your neighborhood is to take a church and community survey. I will talk more in depth about conducting a local survey when I discuss developing an evangelistic strategy later in this chapter. Suffice it to say, if you really want to know what is going on in the community and how to address cultural needs, then simply ask. People do not mind telling you what is on their hearts and minds if they are approached in the right way. And, the information is not only free but invaluable in developing an evangelistic strategy for the local church.

Aside from taking a cultural assessment of your local area, Rick Warren also recommends taking a spiritual evaluation as well.[7] So, you might ask yourself, "What is the spiritual background of those in this community?" While demographic information may give you part of the picture, I am also an advocate of getting to know your neighbors and their spiritual preferences. In my own neighborhood, we have one of the largest Episcopal churches in the United States literally right around the corner from our home. And, less than a quarter mile away, there is an extremely large Roman Catholic parish that many in our community belong to as well.

In my former settings in North Carolina and Georgia, the Southern Baptist Church was very strong and dominated the spiritual landscape. And, in these changing times, if you live in a cosmopolitan city, you will probably find Muslims, Hindus, Orthodox, Mormons and virtually every religion known to humankind. So, what is the advantage of knowing the spiritual background of your community? Primarily, such knowledge will inform your evangelistic strategy to reach others for Christ. For example, if you live in a predominantly Muslim community, perhaps your church should offer a basic course about dialoguing with those of that faith background. It is embarrassing that some Christians know so little about other religions, yet, we sometimes expect them to know so much about ours! Be informed. Educate yourself about the spiritual perspective of others in your neighborhood. Gone are the days when one could simply live in his or her spiritual bubble.

Let's say that you have taken an assessment of the spiritual background of your area and most people are non-Christian. In some parts of Europe and the western United States, most studies indicate that less than ten percent of people are Christians and belong to a church. This religious trend appears to be spreading eastward and even impacting the so-called southern Bible belt. So, how does your church address a community that is largely pagan? We'll talk a little bit more about this issue when we discuss developing an evangelistic strategy. However, a word needs to be said here.

Perhaps, you offer community classes that invite seekers with spiritual questions to explore them within the walls of your church. Some young people are very interested in spiritual matters but don't feel the freedom to explore those within the confines of the church building. Another viable option is to change your worship services so that they are more friendly to non-Christians. Using a ton of religious jargon in services can really throw off non-believers. Keep the language and the service simple. Plug in some great music (the style often played in restaurants or bars in your area), and a Biblical message that is relevant to the lives of those in your neighborhood and you might just see a difference in your ability to touch the community. And, be sure to get outside the church walls. Offer a "Blessing of the Animals" in your local park. Hold a worship service outside the building on occasion when possible. When I was on staff at a large church outside of Atlanta, Georgia, we offered a service called "Lakeside." The service was held on church property, as we were adjacent to Lake Sidney Lanier. From Memorial Day to Labor Day, those services were packed by many people in our community. And, just think, our efforts were consistent with the gospel story. Jesus often preached by the lake. In fact, the gospels paint a portrait of Him speaking out in the community more than within the walls of the synagogue! We could take a lesson from that!

Finally, as your church leadership targets its evangelism efforts, you might consider what Warren calls "personalizing your target."[8] His team at Saddleback Church in California devised a mythical person they called "Saddleback Sam." They described Sam in vivid detail, after researching local geography and demographics, doing cultural studies, and exploring the spiritual mindset in their area. You see, Warren and his leadership team realized when they formed a new church that no one church can reach everyone. So, if your church cannot reach everyone, who will you reach?

Several years ago, I was the pastor of a small church outside of Atlanta. Shortly after I arrived, we did a membership audit and discovered that the church had ninety on roll. Before my arrival, the department of transportation had built a new highway nearby that bypassed the church. As a result, we were virtually invisible to the community and had very limited financial resources. The situation looked rather hopeless as membership continued to dwindle before I arrived. Their last pastoral situation had been a huge disappointment and the leadership was antsy.

One day, several months into my pastorate there, as I was in prayer and study, the Holy Spirit prompted me to meet with the church leadership and figure out what one thing we could all rally around that would motivate the people and move them forward. After meeting with them one afternoon, we came to a clear conclusion: let's put together an outstanding children's ministry. After all, we had a pretty solid core group of children. We even chose Matthew 19:14 as our theme. It is the verse where Jesus says, *"Let the little children come to me, and do not stop them; for it is to such as these that the kingdom of heaven belongs."* Friends, we prayed over the children's ministry at that church and what happened over the next year at that church was nothing short of remarkable. That year, we added several new families to our church so that we showed a ten percent growth rate. At the same time, our children's ministry leader became so passionate about what she did that a few years later she quit her job and entered into full-time ministry. Another parent of one of the children began stepping up and helping in worship services. I mentored him and he got involved in the process to become a pastor in our denomination. Later, he became the pastor of that church and has been there for several years now. I received word recently that he had led the church in burning up the mortgage note on their building after it had been paid in full. Another teenager who helped in our children's ministry later received a call to enter full-time youth ministry. And, why did all this happen? I believe it was because we focused our ministry to be good at something rather than trying to do everything. But, more importantly, it is because we were obedient to the voice of the Holy Spirit to do what God was calling us to do in that setting. Did that little church become a mega-church? No, it did not. But, did we make a difference in that community for Jesus' sake? Yes, we did.

DEVELOPING YOUR CHURCH'S EVANGELISTIC STRATEGY

As you develop your church's unique evangelistic strategy, keep in mind that the next member of your church will likely reflect most of those people already present in your congregation. In other words, if most of the members of your church are white collar professionals and African-American, then you will best be able to reach others like them for Christ.

While some churches do have multicultural ministries that reach large numbers of people, most pastors and leaders will find it easier to reach those that reflect their existing membership. So, as you develop your evangelistic strategy, keep this important principle in mind. It is not that you cannot reach someone who does not reflect your existing membership, but the law of magnetism says that "like attracts like."

Another critical matter to keep in mind as you develop an evangelistic strategy for your church is the leadership component. Rick Warren asks, "What is the cultural background and personality of our church's leadership?"[9] Simply put, people attracted to your church must feel some affinity or common ground with those in leadership. In other words, if guests come to your church and they cannot relate to the pastor, then they are less likely to come back. Your church's leadership must be the bridge that encourages others to cross over into the congregation. In my own pastoral experience at small churches, I have discovered that if people in the community do not like those on the leadership team, regardless of how much they like me as the pastor, they are unwilling to give our church a try. In the best case scenario, people will be attracted to both the pastor and the leadership team and will be more likely to be part of your church's life. So, as you develop your church's leadership strategy, ask yourself if people like your pastor and the leadership team. Often, it takes a long hard honest look at this issue to discover why guests return to your church or not.

Another key idea for developing your church's evangelistic strategy may involve taking a community survey. Such surveys can help you determine what the needs of the community are and how your church might address those needs. Too often, churches simply start doing evangelistic ministries without ever questioning whether or not their strategies are effective. In business, marketing and outreach strategies are evaluated by whether or not one's organization grows and moves forward. However, when it comes to spiritual matters, some people think that just because their church is "doing things," then their ministries are successful. Sometimes, evangelistic ministries are carried out under the banner of "tradition" or simply because it brings the faithful "together." But, the bottom line in evangelism is, "Are we reaching the community in the name of Jesus and winning hearts for Him?" If you want to know how to reach your community for Jesus Christ, then you might want to go ask them their needs and hopes.

In his book, *The Purpose Driven Church*, author, Rick Warren, has a model for a community survey. When he started Saddleback Church in Orange County, California, he took to the streets and asked the community their impressions so that they could develop a strategy for reaching those around them. Such questions as: "What do you think is the greatest need in this area?" and "If you were looking for a church to attend, what kinds of things would you look for?" are poignant, while also giving key insights about reaching the local neighborhood.[10]

Your church can develop its own survey by simply asking the community what it thinks. If you carry out such a survey, it is important to train interviewers to ask the same set of questions to a large variety of people. And, the interviewers should also be people who are bold enough to ask someone they do not know to take a survey. Inevitably, some people will refuse to take any survey at all, so don't be alarmed if you get a few people who say "no." In our experience interviewing people, it is best to survey people in a local park or anywhere else that they are simply hanging out and relaxed. Intruding on someone else's privacy when they are engaged in another activity almost always leads to a "no" when asked to take a survey. Approach people, make eye contact, and smile. And, be sure to introduce yourself. Who wants to take a survey from someone whose name they do not know?

I typically approach someone to take a survey with these words, "Hi, I am Jimmy Jones and I am taking a church and community survey. I am from First Church and wanted to get your thoughts on our neighborhood. I promise that it will only take a couple of minutes to take the survey. Is that okay with you?" I find that it pays to be genuine and up front. Some people may suspect that you are selling something or that your survey will take ten or fifteen minutes. Thus, they will be less likely to participate. So, be sure to make it clear that you value their opinion and their time. Nowadays, people's time is in short supply and a well thought out, brief survey will yield better results than something that is long and drawn out. When someone refuses to take a survey, I always say, "Sure, I appreciate you considering it" and then quickly move on. I don't try to badger people or force them into doing something they don't want to do. After all, we are trying to connect people to Jesus, not turn them off. And, when someone takes the survey and it is completed, I always say, "Thanks so much for your time. Have a great day."

At times, we have even handed out bottled water to people who took the survey. The bottled water has a sticker with our church information and website on it. Such a simple gesture is appreciated by people. We have even handed out snacks in the park to those who completed the survey. Sometimes, people are amazed that the church is actually handing out items in the community. In a sense, that is sad because churches should be known for being some of the most generous people in the world. After all, we serve a generous Savior, don't we?

So, what kinds of questions should a church include on a survey? It really depends on what you are actually planning to accomplish, but these questions below are basic ones that most any church might consider:

1. If you could name one or two of the most important issues facing our community here, what would they be?

2. How do you think our church could help address that issue?

3. If you were to attend a worship service at a church in the area, what would you look for? (a good message, good music, etc.) What would be the most important factor that would take you back to that worship service again?

4. Do you have a favorite radio station? What is it?

5. If you were to give a local church one important piece of advice, what would it be?

Question one above focuses on the most important issue facing the community at the time of the interview. Perhaps, the issue is unemployment or crime. Or, perhaps, there is nothing going on for children or youth in your neighborhood. Your outreach team might consider how your church could address such issues given the answers to the first question above. Should you start a career counseling ministry? Should you spearhead a neighborhood watch ministry? Perhaps, your church could sponsor a community night for children or teenagers in your area. Let the survey give you some guidance.

The third question above highlights your church's worship ministry. Some people in your community will definitely associate the church with worship. For some churches, worship will be the main entry point for reaching people in your area. So, it pays to take a moment to get the community's insights about worship. After all, if you are doing effective outreach in the community but your minister is boring people to tears with the sermon, then it will be tough for your church to move forward.

The fourth question may perplex some people at first. After all, what difference does it make what radio station people listen to? Actually, it can make a lot of difference in the church's outreach ministry. In other words, if many people in your area listen to classic rock and you have a traditional service that relies heavily on classical music, then you are not likely to reach large numbers of folks in your area. And, imagine if you live in an area where people predominately listen to classical music but you are offering hard core heavy metal in your services. Once again, your results will probably be less than satisfactory for your outreach team. Music is a powerful part of people's lives in these changing times and what music your church offers will certainly impact who you can reach in your community.

Finally, make sure that you are prepared to hear people's responses to the fifth question. Believe me, some people that you interview will be amazed that the church even cared to ask what people in the community think. Interviewers should especially encourage people to be honest and bold when answering this question. I always encourage people to tell me exactly what they think, regardless of whether they think I will like it or not. At times, people will open up and talk for quite a few minutes. That is good. Just listen. In fact, one of the real gifts of taking a community survey is that church leaders have an opportunity to listen to people in the community.

Often, church leaders spend so much time with the pastor and each other that they have no idea how the community feels about various issues. But, in these changing times, we must prepare ourselves to listen to those around us or else they will never darken our doors. The new church of the twenty-first century will be a learning community that is devoted to meeting the changing needs of the surrounding community. In fact, your church might want to consider doing the survey on an annual basis to make sure that you are in touch with the emerging trends in your area. Demographical information and statistics will only take you so far. Be willing to listen to your community or risk having an irrelevant church that is not in touch with changing neighborhoods.

CHURCH-WIDE EVANGELISM

As your church develops its evangelistic outreach strategies from the community surveys, it should consider ministries that will reach people in larger venues and settings. According to Mark Mittelberg at Willow Creek Church in South Barrington, Illinois, churches should consider "Innovating High-Impact Outreach Ministries and Events."[11] In other words, after asking what the community is looking for in a survey, church leaders should ask themselves how to reach large numbers of people through large events targeting those who do not know Christ. Perhaps, the best historic example of a high impact evangelistic event in our own culture would be a Billy Graham Crusade. Graham's crusades strategically targeted large numbers of people in outdoor venues and other creative settings. Of course, the success of Graham's outreach efforts cannot be understated. He is perhaps the greatest evangelist of the twentieth century. Graham's influence is felt far and wide and many people have come to know Christ personally as a result of these large crusades.

So, how is your church reaching large numbers of people? What high impact evangelistic events does your church hold to reach the lost? Of course, your church may not be reaching thousands of people at a time like a Billy Graham crusade, but, are you reaching hundreds or even scores of people with the gospel? How does a church go about organizing a high impact event that will reach large numbers of people? First, Mittelberg recommends that church leaders should "define your goals and purpose."[12] Several years ago, I was on staff at a large church in northeast Georgia. Our evangelistic team decided to team up with our children's ministry group to co-sponsor a high impact event to reach children and their parents for Christ. Our goal and purpose was clear: we wanted to present the gospel message to the children and have them make a choice to accept Christ into their hearts. We invited a Christian magician to do a show that presented the gospel story through the medium of magic. The results were outstanding. Some children committed their lives to Christ that afternoon. Mittelberg also writes that churches should have a "target" for their high impact events.[13] Our target was children. Nowadays, in these changing times, it is often true that children take their parents to church rather than the other way around. We felt targeting children was the best way to reach both them and their parents.

Mittelberg goes on to say that churches doing large scale events should also "innovate outside the box."[14] In these changing times, creativity counts. Many children and parents who attended the magic show commented that they had never been to such an event. The format provided a safe, fun, and creative way to reach our community for Christ. And, it was also a lot of fun!

Another important step in holding a high impact event is to "promote your event with precision and power."[15] We did a lot to promote our event. In addition to encouraging church members to invite their friends and neighbors, we also put flyers out in preschools in the community. Many preschools in the area were more than willing to help us promote the event and it was also an inexpensive way to get the word out. And, since there was no charge for the event, we did not exclude any children based upon their ability to pay. We made sure that people in our neighborhood knew that it was a fun and free event that targeted young children. Your team of church leaders and pastors should pray for these high impact events. Of course, this might possibly be the most important step of all. The best human planning must fall subject to God's Holy Spirit when organizing and putting on large scale events. Teams should pray that lost people will be reached. It has been said that prayer moves both God and people. You might even consider having individuals in your church pray for two or three others in their own community who do not know Jesus. As a result of praying, your people may even invite those two or three people or families to attend the event with them. That way, your prayers are lifted for certain individuals.

Finally, after you have held your high impact event, Mittleberg counsels that church leaders "Measure and evaluate results and improve next time."[16] Unfortunately, this is an area where many church teams fail. Often, churches do not look at the results of their efforts and simply do the same events from year to year without considering whether they are really reaching people for Jesus Christ. The results are often tragic. Annual events are often held out of "tradition" or simply because "we just enjoy getting together," rather than considering the eternal consequences of them. Shortly after the high impact event, teams should get together to discuss the results and consider planning for next year.

PERSONAL EVANGELISM: ANOTHER TOOL IN THE CHURCH'S EVANGELISTIC ARSENAL

While high impact church events are important for reaching large numbers of people for Christ, leadership teams should also consider equipping people to do personal evangelism. Therefore, pastors such as Mark Mittelberg of Willow Creek recommend training people to do faith sharing. Too often, pastors and leadership teams assume that all believers are gifted for and know how to share the gospel with others. Unfortunately, sometimes the opposite is the case. However, studies consistently show that many people who come to Christ did so because someone they knew led them to Jesus. So, evangelism training is absolutely essential to a healthy church's outreach ministry.

Recently, the best book that I have read on personal evangelism is Bill Hybels', *Just Walk Across the Room*. As the senior pastor of Willow Creek Church in Illinois, Hybels' church has reached hundreds of people with the gospel of Jesus Christ. It has grown at a healthy pace and is currently one of the most influential in the entire nation. In this groundbreaking book on personal evangelism, Pastor Hybels writes, "...the absolute highest value in personal evangelism is staying attuned to and cooperative with the Holy Spirit."[17] The quote is a powerful reminder that the Holy Spirit is the premier evangelist. God's Spirit is always going before us to draw others to Jesus Christ. And, the Holy

Spirit empowers us to do the work of evangelism in Jesus' name. So, what are some of the key steps in carrying out personal evangelism? In *Just Walk Across the Room*, Hybels gives three: "developing friendships, discovering stories, and discerning the next steps."[18]

The first step in personal evangelism is to "develop friendships." Hybels says that believers should spend time developing rapport with the people around them who do not know Christ. Sadly, he cites a study that shows the longer a person attends church, the fewer evangelistic conversations they engage in with those around them.[19] That is truly sad. Those who should know God the best should share that good news with those who know Christ the least. As believers, God calls us to make an intentional effort to build relationships with those who are unsaved. In Jesus' own ministry, He was criticized for hanging out with prostitutes, tax collectors and "other sinners." Can anyone accuse you and other church leaders of that? If not, then you should begin to develop relationships with a network of people in your life who do not know Christ. And, before you try to win them to Christ, first sit down and get to know them as individuals.

Nowadays, one powerful tool for getting to know others is to simply listen to them. Too often, we are too busy to engage others in deep conversation. However, God calls each one of us to reach out to the lost any way possible. Listen. Dialogue. Connect with them. Then, connect them to Christ.

A second step in practicing personal evangelism is to "discover stories." Hybels refers to the process of "getting near people who are far from God" by an interesting phrase – "the potential of close proximity."[20]

As we get near people, we are called to hear their stories before we share ours. Unselfishly hearing another's story not only affirms the one who shares it, but also gives some hints and ideas about how to reach that non-believer for Christ. Several years ago, I was working at an upscale golf club near Atlanta, Georgia. During that time period, I met a guy who was a flaming non-believer. There were times that his language made my hair curl (and, believe me, there was very little of it then also!). However, as we played golf together and our relationship developed over the course of three years, he began asking me about my faith walk. Eventually, one morning, while we were having breakfast together in a public restaurant, he even asked me to pray before a meal. In the beginning of our relationship, he would not have ever considered praying before a meal! However, it took three years to get to that point. So, there are times when we have to be very patient as we develop friendships and discover other people's stories.

One interesting outcome of that relationship was that I met another couple and invited them to church. They came and eventually became active members of our church…all because I did not give up on an unbeliever. God reminded me through that three year relationship that Jesus does not give up on us so we should not give up on others!

A final step in personal evangelism involves discerning the next steps in your relationship with another person. Once again, the key involves allowing the Holy Spirit to lead you. Is the person ready to commit to Christ? If so, then lead him in a prayer to Jesus Christ asking for forgiveness which opens him up to the new faith life. Or, do you need to back off and allow the person some space in the relationship? There are times when we are working so hard to win someone to Christ that we are not allowing the Holy Spirit to do His work on his or her heart. At those times, simply take a break and approach the individual again when you believe he or she is more open to dialogue. The point is, through prayer and the guidance of God's Holy Spirit, we should always allow God to lead us as we engage with non-believers. As the Lord's prayer says, *"not my will, but thine be done."*

KEY THOUGHTS ON 21ST CENTURY EVANGELISM

Imagine that your church has targeted its evangelism approach. Your leadership team has developed strategies for reaching those in your community. You have taken a survey and have begun to reach your neighborhood through high impact events and training people to practice personal evangelism. And, the results are bearing fruit. Newcomers begin attending your services. However, you notice that these guests come and go as if in a hotel with a revolving door. The pastor and church leaders are tempted to chalk it all up to the lack of commitment in today's world. But, could it be something else?

In order for your church's evangelistic strategies to be successful, you must be willing to follow through by being good hosts to those who attend. Once, I attended a church near our home at the encouragement of a neighbor. During the entire two hour visit, only two people spoke to me. I said "hello" to two other people who did not even speak. Too often, churches have become social clubs that exclude newcomers. Of course, excluding guests is often unintentional on the church's part. However, churches must learn to be more intentional about greeting newcomers. An information table, greeters, and others designated to recognize new church guests can go a long way in making someone new feel welcomed.

Another way that churches may exclude newcomers is through their theological beliefs and practices that are not grounded in scripture. In his book, *They Like Jesus But Not The Church*, pastor, Dan Kimball, writes that non-believers are reluctant to attend church because people there are "judgmental and negative."[21] He points out that people outside the church often know what we stand against rather than what we stand for. I am continually amazed when I listen to sermons that criticize and cast stones at the "outside world" while offering little hope of change to both believers and a hurting world. In the New Testament, Jesus constantly affirms that believers must be individually approached and encouraged to change their errant behavior. In Matthew 18:15, Jesus says, *"If another member of the church sins against you, go and point out the fault when the two of you are alone. If the member listens to you, you have regained that one."* Jesus offers hope to a lost and hurting world. In contrast, some modern day preachers and messages offer little hope to unbelievers. We are called to be people of hope, not people of judgment and negativity. Pastor Dan Kimball writes, "The church is a positive change agent, loving others as Jesus would."[22] Offering people hope in a world that is hurting is one major way to reach newcomers who attend church services. Think about your church's worship services. Do the messages, dramas, and music offer hope to those who attend? Or, has your church become just another agent of guilt that makes people feel spiritually dry and hopeless?

Aside from being "judgmental and negative," another major criticism leveled against the church is that pastors and church leaders teach that "all other religions are wrong."[23] Pastor and author, Dan Kimball explains that "We live in a post-Christian culture."[24] In fact, nowadays, while Christianity is declining in Europe, that trend is also starting to show up in North America. Kimball recommends that churches and leaders should train their people to understand other world faiths and explain why not all paths lead to God. So, when is the last time your church held a seminar on world religions to equip your people for dialoguing with non-believers? In these changing times, in a pluralistic culture, we must equip our people to make an apology for the Christian faith. Rather than merely stating that all other religions are wrong, we must prepare our churches and leaders to know why all other religions are wrong. Informed church leaders and pastors can then have an impact on the world around them.

Finally, as churches and leaders embark on twenty-first century evangelism, they should use a team approach. In the old days, churches hired an evangelism minister who performed visitation duties and coordinated evangelism ministries in isolation. In the new church, pastors and church leaders will train and equip everyone to do the work of evangelism and outreach. Even though some studies report that only ten percent of people in churches actually have the gift of evangelism, everyone should be encouraged, equipped, and reminded to reach out to the lost wherever they are. After all, it is not rocket science! While having special classes for evangelism does help, it also pays to weave evangelistic ideas and reminders into Sunday messages. Moreover, having an evangelistic spokesperson with a passion for reaching the lost is helpful. Ideally, I believe that the evangelistic point person should be someone who is not clergy. People expect pastors to be an advocate for evangelism. However, when a church leader gathers a team of like-minded evangelistic people around, there is nothing that cannot be done. The first evangelists that Jesus gathered around Him were from all walks of life: fishermen, a physician, a tax collector, and others skilled in business and finance. None of them were clergy! And, the most successful church planter in history was a tent maker. Truly, it takes those from common stock to reach each other. That is why people are best at reaching those closest to them: relatives, those they work or live around, and friends. Simple evangelism is perhaps the most effective: reach those you know the best. Modern day studies reveal that we are most successful at reaching those with whom we already have a relationship.

SUMMARY

My wife and I live near the coast in northeast Florida. Last summer, one evening in particular was absolutely perfect for surf fishing. I really enjoy it, so I headed out with some frozen shrimp and two rods. As I made my first cast on a beautiful June evening, I knew what I was fishing for. During the summer in northeast Florida, about all you can expect to catch is a shark or some Whiting. Occasionally, you do catch something else, such as a catfish, but generally speaking your options are limited. I certainly did not expect to catch a Bluegill or a Bass. If I had wanted to do that, I would have gone to a freshwater lake nearby. The results were about what I expected under perfect conditions: I caught two shark and two Whiting. And, of course, the biggest fish got away!

Just as I targeted catching shark and Whiting last summer in our local surf, so churches must target their evangelism strategies. Churches should ask themselves, "Who are we best poised to reach?" Author and pastor, Rick Warren, advocates that churches should identify their targets geographically, demographically, culturally, and spiritually. Next, after pastors and leaders have specifically defined their targets, they should develop a strategy for reaching them. Developing your church's evangelistic strategy will involve taking a serious look at your pastor and leadership team. In addition, it may also be helpful to devise a survey to reach those in your community. After all, demographic information and statistics can only tell you so much. Nothing beats getting out and finding out what is going on in your community. Too often, the church culture is so divorced from its immediate neighborhood that it becomes difficult to reach those nearest your doors.

Another facet of evangelism that we explored in this chapter was church wide evangelism. Your church should have a plan for hosting large impact events that connect people in your area to Christ. However, such big events should be supplemented by personal evangelism. Studies consistently show that most people who attend churches do so on the arms of someone else. There is no substitute for simple invitations to receive Christ or connect with the church through personal relationships. However, churches and leaders should equip people to carry out evangelism in their daily lives by "developing relationships, discovering stories and discerning the next steps," as Bill Hybels puts it.

Finally, I ended this chapter by looking at key thoughts on the topic as we embark on a new century. Plainly stated, churches must learn to be better hosts for newcomers attending services and events. In addition, pastors and church leaders should be less judgmental and negative. Furthermore, we should prepare our people to understand other world religions and equip them to understand why Jesus is the only true path to God. As we do, it will take teams of evangelists to reach a spiritually hurting and dying world in these changing times.

Chapter 6

MINISTRY AND MISSIONS

Evangelism works hand in hand with another important area of church health, and that is, ministry and missions. Scripture commands us to be involved in ministry and missions. Beyond that, ministry and missions should be a natural outflow of our love for Christ. Indeed, ministry and missions often go along with evangelism, since serving is an opportunity to witness for Christ who transforms our hearts and minds when we give our lives to Him.

In chapter six, we will first take a look at the Biblical basis for ministry and mission. The church's outreach ministries, as well as its local and global missions, have a firm foundation in scripture. Next, as the chapter unfolds, we will take a look at gift based ministry and mission teams and their role in the local church. Such gift based ministry teams give people an opportunity to live out their calling to be in ministry and mission. However, it is important for people to find the right "fit" when it comes to service.

According to 1 Corinthians 12:4-5: *"Now there are varieties of gifts, by the same Spirit; and there are varieties of service, but the same Lord."* In other words, we all may offer a unique ministry to the world, but it is the same God Who inspires every one. As the chapter continues, I will examine some keys to developing healthy ministry teams within the life of the church.

Finally, the chapter will conclude with a discussion of growing your ministry and mission team's faith over the long haul. While some ministry teams come and go, a healthy church will sustain strong ministries over the long haul.

THE BIBLICAL BASIS FOR MINISTRY AND MISSION

In Acts 1:8, Jesus says these important words just before He ascends into Heaven: *"But you will receive power when the Holy Spirit has come upon you; and you will be my witnesses in Jerusalem, in all Judea and Samaria, and to the ends of the earth."* Imagine that you have a powerful patriarch or matriarch in your family who is in his or her final dying moments. If that one had the ability to gather his or her thoughts, do you think that one's last words would be important? Of course, they would.

Devoted family members enjoy honoring their loved one's final wishes. Jesus' final wish for the church is that we would be His "witnesses in Jerusalem, Judea, and Samaria, and to the ends of the earth." Let's take an in-depth look at this important statement for a moment.

First, the verse explains that we will receive power from the Holy Spirit to be Christ's witnesses. That is good news! We are not sent out in isolation as we engage the world in ministry and mission. Rather, the Holy Spirit empowers us for the work of God. Human strength by itself is unable to sustain the momentum to perform God's ministry and mission on a continual basis. But, with the power of God, we can do all things through Christ.

Next, Acts 1:8 points out that we are to be Christ's witnesses. So, how did Christ witness? He witnessed to God in both word and deed. If we are to be effective healthy witnesses for Jesus, then we, too, must serve Him in word and deed. In these changing times, words alone are insufficient to witness to Christ. Nowadays, nonbelievers are more impressed by what we do, rather than what we say. A popular adage says, "people don't care how much you know until they know how much you care." Finally, the verse here in Acts also gives us the location where we are to witness. In Jesus' words here in Acts 1:8, there is a movement from the local area (Jerusalem) to worldwide (the ends of the earth). Unfortunately, some churches have no problem being Christ's witnesses in ministry and mission far away from home. However, when it comes down to being involved in your neighbor's problems right around the corner, believers hesitate. That is a shame! Of course, it is wonderful to take a mission trip to a foreign destination because it shakes us out of our cultural comfort zones. But, taking a mission trip down the streets of our cities and neighborhoods sometimes presents a different challenge altogether.

Healthy churches will develop a healthy membership that will want to be engaged in ministry and mission both home and abroad. One mission field is not enough. It takes work at both the local and global fronts for a church to fully live out Jesus' words in Acts 1:8 to touch both Jerusalem (one's local area) and the ends of the earth (global mission). While pastors and church leaders often complain that only a few of their people willingly participate in ministry and mission, Rick Warren notes in *The Purpose Driven Church* that forty percent of all members have contacted a church, or expressed an interest, but have never been asked or do not know how.[1] Furthermore, he cites the Biblical foundation for ministry and mission by saying that believers are called (1 Peter 2:9-10), gifted (1 Peter 4:10), commanded (Matthew 20:26-38), needed (1 Corinthians 12:27), and rewarded (Colossians 3:23-24) for it.[2] So, how do we get our people motivated and prepared to do ministry and mission? Let's take a look.

FINDING THE RIGHT "FIT" FOR YOUR PEOPLE

Perhaps, too often, church pastors and leaders plug people into the wrong ministry and then complain when they quit participating in it. In many of those cases, the person has not really been evaluated to determine what ministry or mission is the best fit for that individual. If you walked into a retail store to buy a pair of shoes, one of the first questions a salesperson would ask you is "What size are you?" Your answer to that inquiry would help the salesperson figure out the best fitting shoe for you. Likewise, churches must take that first step to access a person's best ministry fit before deploying them to their God-given purpose.

Some churches now offer the equivalent of a "New Member Class" that helps plug people into a new church setting. In my estimation and experience, a new member class is the best time to plug people into ministry and mission. At that point in the individual's spiritual journey, he or she is more open to change and new adventure. Thus, it is the perfect time to allow people to become more involved in the church's life. For those who have been church members for years but have not been active in ministry and missions, they too should be given an assessment to determine their best fit.

Another short-term class could be offered for those who have attended church for years. Such a class would challenge them to use their spiritual gifts in ministry and mission for the world. A special session could also be offered within a small group setting to remind its members of the calling that disciples have to be in ministry and mission both locally and globally.

The first step towards assessing someone's spiritual gifts for ministry and mission would be to give him or her an inventory. Fortunately, on the market today, there are a variety of spiritual gifts inventories available. I especially like the spiritual gifts inventory from Injoy. Spiritual gift inventories are an objective means of determining what someone's gifts are. Furthermore, the concept of spiritual gifts itself is a Biblical one. There are many passages in the Bible that speak to the variety of spiritual gifts including 1 Corinthians 12 and Romans 12. Such verses remind us that there are a variety of spiritual gifts, but that each one is inspired by one Holy Spirit. Of course, there are no right or wrong answers to a spiritual gifts inventory. Since God made us all unique, the inventory outcome is always acceptable and a part of God's plan for our lives. However, the top ranking spiritual gifts should also be supplemented by a knowledge of one's heart, abilities, personality, and experiences.

Therefore, in addition to assessing one's spiritual gifts through an inventory, churches should also consider people's hearts, abilities, personalities, and experiences. At the Saddleback Church in Orange County, California, Warren and his team use the acronym "S.H.A.P.E." to help people discover their talents for ministry and mission.[3] The "S" stands for spiritual gifts, the "H" represents heart, the "A" connotes abilities, the "P" symbolizes personality, and the "E" is for one's experiences. So, after helping someone discover their spiritual gifts, the Saddleback Church believes in taking these other aspects into consideration. It is not a bad idea, since one's top one or two gifts may represent an area where he or she does not care to serve. For instance, several years ago, a member of a church where I served took a spiritual gifts inventory and "teaching" tested out as her top gift. However, since she taught school for a living she preferred to use another gift. So, we took a look at where her heart was calling her into ministry and mission. Heart refers to "passion" and represents our areas of enthusiasm and effectiveness.[4] She felt she had a heart for missions and began leading a missions team. It turned out to be a perfect fit. When I left the church, she was thriving as a mission leader in the church.

At other times, pastors and church leaders will consider a person's ability in addition to their spiritual gifts inventory. Occasionally, someone may take a spiritual gifts inventory but not have the talent to carry out their top two or three gifts with excellence. In those cases, churches will have to seriously consider the person's ability. After all, age, physical impairments, mental challenges and other complications may preclude certain individuals from fulfilling their top two or three gifts from an inventory. Have such persons been asked, "What natural abilities and talents do you have?" I once knew a youth in one of our churches who had superior mechanical abilities. He now uses his spiritual gifts to help the church maintain its van and bus. It is absolutely amazing how many ministries a church can sponsor given its people's abilities and talents.

In addition to natural abilities, church leaders and pastors should also take their people's personalities into consideration. We are all born with a unique personality that shapes who we are and how we see the world. Imagine God's fingerprint on your life: there never has, nor will there ever be again, anyone like you on the face of the earth. Traveling to a foreign destination or visiting with people from other cultures gives you a sense of the variety that God created. And, as you match people with ministries and missions, you will certainly want to take their personalities into consideration. While some people may test out on an inventory as being outgoing, it's difficult to completely assess someone's unique personality.

Recently, in a previous church setting, I asked a delightful woman to serve at our hospitality table on Sundays. She did a marvelous job and everyone loved her serving in that capacity. However, there was one major problem: she did not enjoy it. After she had been serving for months in that capacity, she finally admitted to me one day that she had only done it because I had asked her to. Then, she confided that although she appears outgoing, she really prefers to work "behind the scenes." As a result of that honest discussion, she was placed in another outreach ministry where she could make a significant contribution to our church, but in a quiet way. The result was a huge success for both her and the church. We allowed her to serve in a way that matched her personality.

Finally, finding the right fit for people in your church might mean considering their experiences. Life brings many challenges to us through our family life, work, and just experiencing the joys and trials of daily living. I once met a woman in church who had lost two of her children to death early in their lives. Through that painful experience, she was able to begin a ministry to reach couples and individuals who had endured a child's death. Later, I learned about an organization called Compassionate Friends that ministers with parents whose children are deceased. The miracle of Christianity is Easter. In other words, through death comes life. Those who have lost loved ones can be a great support in grief groups for others who have experienced such tragedy. Allowing people to use their experiences to transform the lives of others is a ministry and mission that the church can fully support.

GIFT BASED MINISTRY AND MISSION TEAMS

Now that pastors and church leaders have assessed people for ministry and missions, it is time to put them on a team so that they can soar with their strengths. Jesus always put people on ministry teams. In Luke 10:1, Jesus sends out His followers in pairs to nearby towns and villages. And, the disciples themselves were a team of twelve, with Peter often serving as their leader. Therefore, gift based ministry teams are a Biblical concept, and one that churches would be wise to adopt in these changing times. In my own experience, it is unwise to place someone in a ministry position without the benefit of a team. First of all, doing ministry in isolation is not a Biblical practice. Second, it is unsafe and unwise to use volunteers in isolation.

Nowadays, even volunteer childcare workers and those who work with teenagers should undergo a thorough background screening and fingerprint process. Such prudent practices not only make church guests feel better about leaving their children in your people's hands, but they also ensure that the church is a safe and healthy environment for young ones. Another benefit to working in teams is that people who suffer discouragement can lean on one another. Let's face it, even volunteer ministry and missions have challenges and God does not call us to face those challenges alone.

Each ministry team should have a focus, a team leader and co-leader, and be made up of several team members. So, for instance, someone with a spiritual gift of craftsmanship can be placed on a team where they can be a vital part of that ministry. Again, it is amazing the talent that we have in churches, if people are simply given the chance to perform. In one church I served several years ago, a member of the congregation built a beautiful altar in the church. Honestly, it was one of the best pieces of work I had ever seen...and it was donated to the church!

When people are placed on a ministry team, three things should occur: First, the leader must be willing to hand off projects to others. Too often, some team leaders do things themselves "because it is a hassle to ask someone else" or because they feel they can do it better themselves. However, a team leader must simply facilitate and guide the ministry that is taking place. When the team leader takes it upon him or herself to perform every ministry task, then there is no need for the team and people will start to drift away. In addition, a team leader should also be willing to empower, resource and otherwise support the individual who is engaging in the ministry work. Imagine a team leader gives you a job to do with no resources and no instruction on how to get the job done. At best such work will be delayed and at worst it will not be done at all!

Finally, the team member who successfully completes the work should be recognized in some way. Some churches hold a volunteer banquet each year to recognize those who participate in its ministries and missions. When recognizing those who serve on ministry teams, it is always essential to do it in the way that the person being recognized would appreciate. Some who complete work appreciate little recognition at all. In those cases, a simple verbal "thank you" or note from the team leader is sufficient. In other cases, a project may be so big or so noteworthy that it should be mentioned in church or a public recognition should be planned. It all depends on how the person being applauded would receive it. No one should be embarrassed on the one hand or underappreciated on the other hand. Just take each individual and situation into consideration when saying "thank you."

The really important thing is just to make sure that someone is thanked. Thanking someone not only makes them feel appreciated, but also ensures that they will be willing to help the next time when requested.

KEYS TO DEVELOPING GREAT GIFT BASED MINISTRY TEAMS

So, the pastor and church leaders have identified those with spiritual gifts and placed them on a gift based ministry team. Now, how can they make sure that such groups will continue to thrive in these changing times?

In his book, *Organizing Genius*, author, Warren Bennis, writes, "Every great group has a strong leader."[5] Furthermore, he adds, "The ability to recognize excellence in others and their work may be the defining talent of leaders of great groups."[6] The fact is great ministry and mission teams can only be led by great leaders. If a team is serving and doing great, it is because there is a great leader behind it. Great leaders will empower, resource, and recognize their teams on a continual basis for maximum success.

Aside from having a great leader, the second key to developing a superb ministry team is to recruit the right people. The right group with the right people will go places. In his book, Bennis says that "Recruiting the most talented people possible is the first task of anyone who hopes to create a great group."[7]

Back in the 1970's, I was a huge Cincinnati Reds fan. In 1975 and 1976, they captured back to back World Series titles with an amazing team. Having a great head coach is a huge advantage in sports; however, without great talent and performance, a team will not be a winner. The same is true in church work. A great team leader must be backed by a great team. Putting someone with the wrong gifts on the wrong ministry team frustrates both the team leader and the individual being placed there. That is why recruiting the right people for the right team is so critical.

Finally, another key to crafting an excellent ministry team is to give them a clear and collective purpose. Groups that believe that they are on a divine mission are committed to excellence. Indeed, ministry teams are literally on a mission from God! The important thing is that your ministry team has a clear and compelling purpose that makes everything they do seem valuable. If people sense that you are wasting their time or that the task has little value, it will distract the team from performing at its optimum level. Each team must have members who truly believe that their efforts are making a difference in the world. Remember, pastors and church leaders, your teams are not working for a paycheck. Rather, they are working for a payoff. That is, knowing that their efforts have made a dent in the world. And, of course, there is always the additional benefit of God's eternal reward of Heaven!

GROWING YOUR MINISTRY AND MISSION TEAM'S FAITH IN CHANGING TIMES

Ministry and mission in the twenty-first century is tougher than ever. The church is no longer the center of attention in our neighborhoods and communities. So, pastors and church leaders must learn to have creative visions for their ministry and mission teams in the new century. In his book, *Your Best Life Now*, author and pastor, Joel Osteen, talks about how his dad transformed Lakewood Church (that once met in a feed store) into one of the largest in the nation. Joel urges readers to "enlarge your vision." Churches, along with their ministry and mission teams, must enlarge their visions during these changing times. In this new century, creative imaginative visions will define the church of Jesus Christ. For instance, I once read a newspaper article about the "Recycled Church." The story was about a church in inner-city Jacksonville, Florida, that uses recycled products in its facility, including the sanctuary. The church chooses to use its money to reach out to the community in various ways: afternoon youth programs, a variety of family events, and ministries that target the homeless. In other words, it is not about the building, it is about the ministry and mission of Christ's church. Ministry and mission teams should always be looking for such creative ways of reaching their communities. The new church in these changing times will be characterized by a large vision, not simply a large building.

In addition to enlarging their visions, ministry and mission teams in the new century should also have a commitment to excellence in all that they do. I am amazed, nowadays, at how many churches are content with mediocrity. In fact, some churches have simply come to expect and live with it. However, our Lord does not call us to be mediocre when we serve in His name. Your ministry and mission team should commit to doing its work with excellence and passion. If you are serving barbeque, then serve the best barbeque possible. If you are building a Habitat home, then have a good attitude and provide the best labor possible. If you are serving in a soup kitchen, do it as if you were a waiter in a five star restaurant. When we are doing something for Jesus, we are called to give it our all. In Matthew 25:40, Jesus reminds His hearers, *"Truly I tell you, just as you did it to one of the least of these who are members of my family, you did it to me."* When providing materials for a given project, I also think that you should have the best ones possible. Poor quality materials and a negative attitude sends a non-verbal message that the church is not excited about sponsoring a given event. In short, everything that your mission team does should be done with a passion that reaches for the stars.

Aside from a commitment to excellence, another key to growing your ministry and mission team's faith is to overcome any obstacles in your way to accomplish the given task. How many times have you been tempted to give up on something when you are performing a ministry or mission work? Honestly, as a pastor, I will have to admit that there are times I have been tempted to give up on the ministry itself. But, of course, God's people are called to persevere in the face of challenges. In Luke 18:1-8, Jesus tells the story of the widow facing the unjust judge. The two characters in the parable could not be more different. In those days, widows were penniless and powerless. So, while the widow in the story desires a just verdict against her adversary, she really does not have a leg to stand on against the powerful judge. However, through her perseverance and sheer determination, she is able to achieve the verdict she desires. The morale of the wonderful story here in Luke's Gospel is that perseverance and determination pays off.

Never give up! There will be times that your ministry and mission team is tempted to give up on something that you truly believe God has called you to. Find a way to reach deep within yourselves and accomplish the task. Perseverance will make your ministry and mission team grow stronger.

Finally, as your ministry and mission teams grow in faith, they should be reminded that a major Biblical principle involves sowing and reaping. One miraculous gift of serving on a ministry and mission team within your church is that when you sow blessings into the lives of others, then you, too, will be blessed. While the world teaches that when we give something away, it is gone, the Bible teaches that in giving we also receive. In the Sermon on the Mountain, Jesus' most famous message, He says these words: *"Blessed are the merciful, for they will receive mercy"* (Matthew 5:7). In other words, God (and others) will be merciful to us when we are merciful to others.

Several years ago, I visited a man from our church in the nursing home on a regular basis. During that time period, I got to know his family and business partners very well. He had a wife and no children. In addition, he had some extended family and business friends who were close to him. The man and his wife had been very successful in business and they shared their generosity with those around them on a regular basis. One afternoon, as I was visiting the man and his wife, she asked me to have a prayer with her family. He was near death, and we knew that his time on earth was about to end. The man had not sat up or opened his eyes in days. Immediately after I finished the prayer, the man sat up and opened his eyes. Then, he gave his wife a hug and died in her arms. In all my years as a pastor, I had never witnessed anything quite so beautiful. Meanwhile, my wife and I were in the process of closing on a home in another state and our money was a bit tight. I had not shared our financial circumstances with anyone, but was counting on God to provide our needs. A week or so after the man's funeral, I received an envelope from his widow. After I ripped open the envelope, I noticed that she had sent a thank you card. As I was pulling the small card out of the envelope, a folded check fell on the floor. I read the note and a few moments later I picked up the check. Unfolding it, I saw the amount in the white box…$1000. I nearly fainted. That check helped us tremendously when it came time to close on our new home. In fact, if we had not had it, we probably would not be living in the home where we have now been for several years.

Friends, when you reach out to bless someone else, you will be blessed. Of course, your blessings will not always come in a material way. Sometimes, the greatest blessings are the ones that come in a different way. However, rest assured, you, your ministry and mission team will be blessed when you reach out to bless someone else. God has called us to a blessing; and, in that blessing, we too are blessed.

SUMMARY

Participating in acts of ministry and mission are not an option for the modern day healthy church. Not only is ministry and mission a Biblical mandate, but it is also one that will make your church more culturally relevant in these changing times. Nowadays, people do not care how much the church knows until they know how much the church cares. Ministry and mission are most effective when done both locally and globally. The church that only does one or the other is not fulfilling the Biblical mandate to do mission and ministry in Jerusalem (locally) and to the ends of the earth (globally).

In order to assign people to ministry teams, a spiritual gifts inventory should first be done. As Paul points out in Romans 12 and 1 Corinthians 12, there are a variety of gifts in the church, but God inspires them all through the Holy Spirit. Each spiritual gift is important to the church and helps build up the entire body. A healthy church will consider each person's heart, abilities, personality and experiences along with his or her spiritual gifts when assigning people to gift based ministry teams. These gift based ministry teams also have a Biblical precedent, as Jesus sent out people to mission work in pairs (Luke 10:1). Each team should be led by a strong leader and co-leader and have highly functioning members. In addition, each ministry team must have a clear sense of its mission and purpose in order to be faithful. Finally, over the long haul, teams must have a big vision for their ministries, do their work with excellence, overcome any obstacles, and continue to see the value of sowing blessings into people's lives.

When one blesses another, then he or she is in turn blessed. The cyclical life of team ministry means that sowing into other people's lives will ultimately help Christ grow in their own hearts. Ministry and mission will touch many hearts and lead non-believers to Christ when they witness these loving ministry and mission acts.

Chapter 7

FELLOWSHIP

One of the earliest pictures of a Christian community is found in Acts 2:42. The verse reads that the earliest disciples of Jesus devoted themselves to four things: "the apostle's teaching," "fellowship," "the breaking of bread," and prayer. It is evident from the most ancient Biblical snapshots that fellowship should play a central role in the believer's life. So, what is fellowship? The Greek word for it is *koinonia*, and it connotes intimate community and relationships among believers. Author, Doug Fields, who is the former Lead Student Minister at Saddleback Church in California, notes the following about fellowship:

> "In the early church, fellowship was more relational than recreational. It included sharing (1 John 1:7) and breaking bread (Acts 2:42) with other believers, as well as developing intimacy with Christ (1 Corinthians 1:9) and with other believers (Galatians 2:9). This is a much different image than hanging out with students and playing volleyball."[1]

The Lead Pastor at Saddleback Church, Rick Warren, in his book titled, *The Purpose Driven Life*, simply defines fellowship as "experiencing life together."[2] While some settings have reduced modern fellowship to "having a meal together," the healthy church will embrace the Biblical concept of fellowship and reclaim its benefits.

In this chapter, we will first explore the individual's responsibility in fellowship. In other words, fellowship does not just happen because someone happens to be inside the church walls. Each person has to make a contribution to the larger group. Next, I will make an examination of how to experience fellowship with a healthy church setting. Simply put, healthy fellowship must happen on several levels: the worship setting, in small groups, and with one or more other disciples. Church leaders and pastors must encourage their people to experience healthy fellowship on these three levels. It is my experience as a pastor that if someone falls away from fellowship activities, then he or she is likely to fall away from the church. Fellowship participation can be a good way to gauge someone's relationship with the church. Finally, as the chapter concludes, we will look at how action oriented fellowship can transform believers' lives. We must study, share, serve and suffer together in order for genuine fellowship to occur.

THE BELIEVER'S ROLE IN FELLOWSHIP

In his book, *The Purpose Driven Life*, author Rick Warren notes that real fellowship must begin with "honesty," which may involve speaking the truth with love.[3] That is not a bad way to begin Christian fellowship. In our relationships with others at church, we must first be genuine and open with each other.

One of the primary criticisms leveled against the church by non-believers is that we are "hypocrites." Of course, a hypocrite is someone who says one thing but does another. As believers, we must not cover up our feelings, but speak the truth in love with our fellow Christians. While some churches and small groups will avoid conflict at any cost, it can be a window of opportunity for developing deeper relationships with Christ and each other. Honesty is foundational for fellowship, for without it, there is no genuine love or mutual trust. In order for fellowship to remain healthy and honest, believers must be real with each other and with non-believers. When we complain about each other outside the church walls, but pat each other on the back at church, then we are sending the world a message that we are insincere. In these changing times, one of the greatest qualities of a believer is honesty and genuineness. As a former youth minister, I can attest that kids can see right through you when you are not honest with them. Therefore, honesty and vulnerability are absolutely essential for real fellowship to occur. It is the believer's responsibility to cultivate a sense of honesty and genuineness in his or her relationships with other Christians and non-believers.

Another vital quality in the Christian's fellowship life is humility. I like Rick Warren's definition of humility in *The Purpose Driven Life*: "Humility is not thinking less of yourself; it is thinking of yourself less."[4] As a pastor, I have seen pride rear its ugly head in the church more than once. One of a Christian's biggest temptations is to think that he or she is more holy than others. Typically, these prideful actions take place just before a big fall in someone's faith walk. Satan walks hand in hand with pride. When people begin to think more of themselves than others, it becomes difficult to yield to the Holy

Spirit's guidance of one's life.

When James and John argued over who would sit at the Lord's right hand, Jesus tells them that the *"humble will be exalted and the exalted will be humbled."* If a believer wants to become great, then he or she must first humble one's self at the cross. At one point in my ministry, as I was upwardly mobile as a pastor within our denominational church, my wife and I decided to move. I went from being an associate pastor at a large church in Georgia to being a middle school teacher and then a youth minister. One thing is for sure, if you want to be humbled, just hang out with some kids and teenagers for a while! Anyway, though it took some time, I endured those experiences with some humility and later again renewed my ministerial call by becoming an associate pastor at one of the largest churches in our conference. God certainly has a way of exalting us after we have been humbled!

In addition to honesty and humility, a final component of the believer's Biblical fellowship responsibility is to be there with each other on a regular basis. One thing is for sure, fellowship cannot occur if you are not there! Again, Acts 2:42 says that the early disciples "devoted" themselves to fellowship. That means that even though the weather was right for hanging out on the beach or the Sunday football game was coming on television, those believers were absolutely committed to being with each other!

Of course, my statement above is comical, but it is disheartening that Christians, today, struggle with their fellowship commitments. However, the Bible calls us into fellowship with each other through such passages as Hebrews 10:24-25: *"And let us consider how to provoke one another to love and good deeds, not neglecting to meet together, as is the habit of some, but encouraging one another, and all the more as you see the Day approaching."* Simply put, fellowship must be a priority for the committed believer. It is not a matter of "I am not doing anything else today." Rather, we are called by the Bible and the Spirit of Christ into fellowship with each other. Who knows? Some one else might just miss a blessing because you did not show up at church or your small group today. As a believer, I am often surprised that the Sunday that I did not want to attend church was the Sunday that I received the greatest blessing. Sometimes, God will choose to give you a special blessing just when you least anticipated it. That is simply God's way of teaching us what grace is really all about.

EXPERIENCING FELLOWSHIP WITHIN THE CHURCH SETTING

Perhaps, the most obvious way for a believer to experience fellowship at church is to attend worship services. Most worship settings have all, or nearly all, of the four characteristics of the early Christian gatherings described in Acts 2:42: *"They devoted themselves to the apostle's teaching and fellowship, to the breaking of bread and the prayers."* In modern worship, the scriptures are read and the apostle's teaching is interpreted by a minister who gives a message. As discussed in an earlier chapter, there are other ways to share the apostle's teaching in worship – through music, drama, skits, and other creative arts. Through worship, the apostle's teaching is planted in the heart of a believer and it edifies one's faith walk.

Next, fellowship itself is mentioned. At times, I have heard people say that they do not see the benefit of getting up and going to church. After all, they reason, I can just stay at home and watch it on television. But, unfortunately, it is hard to have fellowship with a bunch of people on your television screen. You don't know their joys and trials. However, when you rub elbows with people at church, you have the opportunity to know them deeper as God's children. Indeed, there is spiritual strength in numbers when we gather and raise our hands in praise to God our Creator. There is just something about being present in worship that blesses the heart and lifts the spirit.

Acts 2:42 also references the phrase "the breaking of the bread." The phrase here means Holy Communion or the Lord's Supper. It is evident from ancient texts that the early church celebrated the holy meal on a regular basis. In the early days, communion was practiced just after the early believers enjoyed a meal together. Of course, Holy Communion recalls Jesus' sacrifice for us and anticipates His second coming. The communion meal is a special and sacred way for us to experience a deep spiritual relationship with God and each other. Indeed, Paul even mentions in 1 Corinthians 11 that we should first be reconciled with our neighbors before we take communion.

And, finally, in Acts 2:42, prayer is mentioned. While private prayer has its assets, there is much to be said for praying with and for other believers. Corporate prayer is a powerful way to experience fellowship with other believers as we intercede for others with the Lord Himself. Corporate prayer represents vertical fellowship with God and horizontal fellowship with each other.

While believers can experience genuine fellowship through

worship, a more intimate setting in one's church is the small group. Small group fellowship is a Biblical practice. In the gospels, Jesus often calls the twelve disciples apart to be with them. During those small group gatherings, Jesus confides in them, empowers them for ministry, and shares table fellowship with them. Through the power of small group fellowship, Jesus transforms these ordinary guys into an extraordinary group of men who changed the face of the earth with their message of grace and love. As I stated earlier in this project, if Jesus had only spoken to large groups and had never invested Himself in a small group, you would probably not even recognize His name today. After His death and resurrection, the small group of disciples continued His ministry and mission successfully, winning hearts and lives for Christ.

In my own church experience, I cannot say enough about how valuable a small group is for Christian fellowship. Just today, I received a call from someone who I was in a small group with five years ago. To this day, we still stay in touch, and visit her on a regular basis when I am able. Small groups are where I have experienced fellowship and spiritual growth in powerful ways. It is the fellowship setting where your heart and mind are truly conformed to the way of Christ. I have witnessed laughter, tears, and heard stories about the transformation of lives in small group. In an earlier chapter, I discussed the importance of small groups and how they add a valuable component to church life. Indeed, small groups are the brick and mortar that hold the church together through heart-warming relationships. If your church setting is struggling with its small group ministry, you will notice a marked decline in fellowship. Moreover, that lack of fellowship will soon impact your larger church setting. Pastors and church leaders, do absolutely everything in your power to sustain, empower and encourage the power of small group ministry in your settings.

Finally, another good way to experience fellowship in your church setting is to meet with a "disciple partner." Your disciple partner may be someone already in your small group, or it may be someone else you know is a strong believer. In the gospels, Jesus often met with an "inner circle" – Peter, James, John. The Lord experienced some of His most intimate moments with those three disciples, including the transfiguration. Within your own small group or larger church fellowship, you will most likely connect with one, two or three individuals with whom you really enjoy. I would encourage you to meet with one or two other people on a regular basis to support, challenge, and encourage each other. For nearly five years, I have met with another pastor in my local area. His friendship and our fellowship has meant a great deal to me. When choosing a disciple partner, I recommend the following guidelines:

-If you are married, it should be someone of the same gender as you; after all, the spiritual intimacy of the relationship could spark romance if you are not careful.

-It should be someone with whom you have a few things in common: vocation, age, life experiences, etc. For example, my disciple partner and I share the same career and calling. We both have young children and we are in the same age category.

-It should be someone who can give you a different perspective on life matters. For instance, your disciple partner should be able to give you healthy and honest advice that you may not have considered.

-It should be someone who will keep your discussions confidential. I would suggest forming a covenant partnership with your disciple partner. In other words, what happens in Vegas, stays in Vegas. If you and your partner do not agree to keep matters confidential, you will probably be less likely to really share trust and spiritual intimacy with each other.

-You should meet together on a regular basis (such as weekly for one hour) and be on time for those meetings. Your meeting with a disciple partner should not merely be a social hour. Rather, you might consider the following questions to guide you:

1. What was the spiritual high point of your week?
2. What was the spiritual low point of your week?
3. When did you feel closest to Christ this week?
4. When did you feel far away from Christ this week?
5. What is your action plan for staying close to Christ in the coming week?

The questions above are merely a general guideline. Your discussions may vary from week to week. In the relationship with my disciple partner, there have been times where I have poured out my heart to him and he said barely anything. At other times, he has poured out his heart to me and I have said little. Life experiences may dictate where the Holy Spirit leads your discussion on a week to week basis. And, at the conclusion of our time together, we always share prayer requests and then pray for each other. Believe me, it is nice to hear someone else praying for you. There are times when others tell me that they are praying for me or the circumstances in my life. But, to actually hear someone else praying for you boosts your spirit.

Conversely, when you pray for someone else, you are given the opportunity to be in ministry with them. I strongly urge you to secure a disciple partner in your own church setting. If not, find another believer outside your church setting with whom to experience fellowship. Remember, Jesus promises in Matthew 18:20, *"For where two or three are gathered in my name, I am there among them."* Writers, Don Clifton and Paula Nelson in their book, *Soar With Your Strengths* observe that "Quality relationships develop one on one."[5] Church leaders and pastors in healthy churches should provide the culture and environment for those relationships to thrive and for fellowship to grow. I urge you to get together with your leaders to discuss how the disciple partner format might work itself out in your own church setting. Plant those relationships, nurture them, and then sit in amazement as they grow before your eyes.

ACTION-ORIENTED FELLOWSHIP IN YOUR CHURCH SETTING

In his book, The Purpose Driven Life, author and pastor, Rick Warren, says that fellowship happens as believers share, study, serve, and suffer together.[6] All four of the above fellowship qualities necessitate that believers be proactive. So, if believers truly want to experience genuine fellowship, then they must be willing to share, study, serve, and suffer together. While worship represents large group fellowship, I believe that sharing, studying, serving, and suffering can best be experienced in the small group and disciple partner settings.

These four qualities may even be viewed as core values of the small group. Mutual sharing in love draws the small group participants together. Studying helps build their minds up in Jesus Christ. You will recall that Jesus challenges us to love God the Father with all our hearts, minds, and souls. The small group environment is an excellent setting to conform your mind to Christ while you experience top notch fellowship. Serving is yet another way for group members to draw closer together. Serving in a soup kitchen, putting boxes together for Operation Christmas Child, and building a Habitat home together are all excellent ways for your small group members to connect with each other at the deepest levels. Finally, fellowship also takes place as we suffer together. In an earlier chapter, I described how one woman who lost her young son was supported by her small group. I have repeatedly heard stories from church members who felt overwhelmed with love when their other small group members supported them during a time of intense suffering in their lives. Such stories remind me that real fellowship is the firm foundation of a healthy church in these changing times.

SUMMARY

Christian fellowship means that individuals in church are experiencing real life together. Fellowship is really the cement that holds the bricks and mortar together for the people called church. At times, those outside the church have even described its purpose as fellowship. However, fellowship does not just happen. Individuals within the church body have to make it happen. Through what Rick Warren calls honesty, humility, confidentiality, and meeting frequency, people within the church will begin to understand what genuine Christian fellowship is all about. The truth is, if an individual is putting little effort into making fellowship happen, then it is probably not going to happen. Experiencing fellowship within the church setting can generally take place in three distinct ways: through worship, the small group setting, and by meeting with a disciple partner. The small group setting continues to be the premier way for people to experience true fellowship.

Finally, as people in church are encouraged to share, study, serve, and suffer together, they will come to know what Jesus, Himself, meant by fellowship. As an old hymn favorite says, *"What a fellowship, what a joy divine, leaning on the everlasting arms."* Fellowship means that we are connected with each other through the amazing grace and blood of our leader, Jesus Christ.

Chapter 8

THE HEALTHY 21ST CENTURY CHURCH

In my experience and study of church health, I have identified four major characteristics that I believe describe a solid Biblical approach to ministry in these changing times. Churches that I have cited in this book, such as Saddleback, Willow Creek, and North Point Community Church are congregations that are strong in each of these four categories. On the other hand, unhealthy churches are weak in one or more of these categories. As we close the project with this chapter, let's take a look at these four characteristics and explore how they impact church health in a new century. I believe that we will find many parallels between church health now and two thousand years ago when Jesus first established it.

Characteristic # 1 – Connecting people to Jesus Christ by fulfilling the Great Commandment and the Great Commission

The healthy church in these changing times will be one that

connects people to Jesus Christ and fulfills both the Great Commandment and the Great Commission. The first and greatest responsibility of any church is to offer people personal salvation through a transforming dynamic relationship with Jesus Christ. The church is in the life transformation business. If people in our churches are not changed by the power of a personal relationship with Jesus Christ then everything else we do is irrelevant. Furthermore, as lives are changed and people begin conforming themselves to the mind, heart, and soul of Jesus Christ, then modern churches will empower them to live out both the Great Commandment and the Great Commission. For Jews in Jesus' day, the law was the centerpiece of their religion. When Jesus was asked by the Pharisees to quote the greatest law out of hundreds of them, He replied: *"'You shall love the Lord your God with all your heart, and with all your soul, and with all your mind.' This is the greatest and first commandment. And a second is like it: 'You shall love your neighbor as yourself.' On these commandments hang all the law and the prophets."*

Therefore, healthy churches do everything in their strength to encourage their people to love God and to love their neighbors. A major way that healthy churches live out the Great Commandment is through their commitment to the Great Commission. In other words, healthy churches don't just love on God and each other. Healthy congregations in these changing times will consider the stranger and the non-believer to be their 'neighbor.' So, Jesus says in Matthew 28:19-20, *"Go therefore and make disciples of all nations, baptizing them in the name of the Father, and of the Son, and of the Holy Spirit, and teaching them to obey everything that I have commanded you. And, remember, I am with you always, to the end of the age."*

Put simply, the twenty-first century healthy church will be absolutely sold out on evangelism. A congregation is a living organism. It either grows or dies. Healthy churches are ones that are committed to new growth. Just as a healthy plant shows new growth and advancement, so a church must constantly be growing through reaching out to newcomers in Jesus' name.

Churches such as Saddleback, Willow, and North Point are absolutely sold out for the purpose of connecting people to Jesus while also fulfilling the Great Commandment and the Great Commission. It is not sheer numbers that make these churches healthy. Rather, it is the strength of their commitment to bringing others into that essential relationship with Jesus Christ that sets them apart.

Characteristic # 2- Numerical Growth

Building upon the essential foundation of a relationship with Jesus Christ, and a commitment to the Great Commandment and the Great Commission, healthy churches in the twenty-first century will also experience numerical growth. Of course, numerical growth, in and of itself, is not an indicator of church health. After all, throughout history, there have been famous cults that have come and gone which were not committed to putting people into a relationship with Jesus Christ. However, when combined with the first characteristic quoted above, numerical growth is also a powerful trait of healthy churches primarily because it is also a Biblical one. Acts 2:41 says that three thousand people responded to Peter's message and were baptized. And, a few verses later, Luke writes, "*…And day by day the Lord added to their number those who were being saved.*" Now that sounds like a healthy church! The Holy Spirit was stimulating numerical growth among the early church believers.

Have you ever been in a church where the numbers were steadily declining? Have you ever looked outside your window at home and seen a tree dying or your yard drying up? Friends, somebody or something that is dying is unhealthy. If a church experiences steady and consistent numerical decline over a period of time there is a sign that something is wrong. Likewise, if a tree, a plant, or grass is dying something must be done before it is too late. Too often, some churches ignore their numerical decline until it is too late. And, at some point, the more you begin declining, the harder it is to stop the trend and begin to increase. It is as if the "domino effect" comes into play as you experience church life together.

On the other hand, a healthy church is one where the numbers increase steadily over time until one healthy church gives birth to another one. According to the Saddleback website (www.saddleback.com), Rick and Kay Warren launched that church in California with just over two hundred members in 1980. Today, the church has several thousand members and more than two hundred active ministries in the area. One in nine people in that area now call Saddleback their church home. Moreover, Saddleback has given birth to other new churches.

And, Willow Creek Church in South Barrington, Illinois? Its website (www.willowcreek.org) reports that it started in the early 1970's out of a youth ministry at a nearby church and has grown to several thousand in attendance each week. You see, people want to come where the Holy Spirit is transforming lives for Jesus Christ. Combined with a commitment to changing lives for Jesus and an adherence to both the Great Commandment and the Great Commission, churches like these are making a real difference in the world.

Characteristic # 3- Making an Impact In and Beyond the Local Setting

In addition to numerical growth, healthy churches also have an impact beyond their local settings. In Acts 1:8, Jesus challenges the disciples to be His "witnesses in Jerusalem (locally), in all Judea and Samaria, and to the ends of the earth (worldwide)." Therefore, our ministries should not be limited to our local geographic settings. Rather, we should share the gospel and its truth worldwide. Unhealthy churches have little influence on their local areas and beyond; in contrast, healthy churches are involved at both the local and global level. Again, let's take a look at Saddleback, Willow, and North Point. Rick Warren's books, *The Purpose Driven Church* and *The Purpose Driven Life,* have had an enormous impact on Christendom and beyond. The mission and ministry efforts of Saddleback have reached many foreign shores. Likewise, Willow Creek Church has had a huge effect on the lives of church leaders and pastors from around the globe. Last year, I had the opportunity to visit a satellite campus here in Jacksonville, Florida, for Willow's Leadership Summit. It was one of the best events I have attended in years and I have put some of those leadership principles into practice. Finally, Andy Stanley, pastor of North Point Community Church in Alpharetta, Georgia, has published several books, launched other new churches and exported his messages and studies to other congregations. While some churches are content to minister to themselves and their membership, healthy congregations will discover creative ways to be in ministry both within and beyond their local areas. Just as the early church reached many parts of Europe and Africa with the gospel, so we, today, should seek to have a worldwide impact.

Characteristic #4- Healthy Churches Pass the Seven Point Inspection

As I close this book, I am convinced that healthy churches in the twenty-first century pass and excel at the seven point inspection. Indeed, for a church to be strong in these changing times, it must be healthy in the seven areas I have covered in the previous seven chapters.

Churches that have this fourth characteristic already have the three traits that I mentioned earlier in the final chapter here. First, healthy churches in the new century are ones that have a strong sense of vision, mission and core values. If your church does not have a clear and compelling vision and mission, it will fail to be a healthy church in the new century. Moreover, its core values should be Biblical and shared by those who form the church.

Second, healthy churches in these changing times should also have strong pastoral leadership. When a church experiences turbulence with respect to pastoral leadership, it will not be a healthy church. Nowadays, changing pastors ever so often ensures that your church will not grow. Your pastoral leader must have a healthy Biblical balance between the personal and professional life. In the third place, healthy churches in modern times also have superior worship that truly connects people to Jesus Christ. Worship that is done half-heartedly or without excellence, does not draw newcomers to services or build up the faithful. Your worship life should be creative, Biblical, relevant and done well in order to pass the healthy church inspection. In addition, your church must have a plan for plugging people into its discipleship ministry. People who get the most out of church do so in small group settings. Is your church's discipleship ministry healthy? Are people studying and serving faithfully in their small group settings? Are your small group leaders strong and trained for leading these disciples?

And, what about your evangelism ministry? Unfortunately, too many churches ignore this area of church health. Your church must be committed to reaching newcomers for the kingdom. A church that is not adding new people is one that is becoming stagnant and will eventually die. Another key element of modern day church health is your congregation's efforts in ministry and mission. Are you sold out to the people beyond your walls? Is your church actively involved in both local and global mission efforts? If not, then your people are becoming an island unto themselves. Healthy churches in these changing times will have relevant ministries that truly touch the hearts and lives of their community and their world.

And, finally, is your church's fellowship ministry healthy? Is Christ the center of your church's fellowship ministry, or has your church just become a place for hanging out? As we embark on this new century, I trust that your church will use the health checkup in this book to guide you towards fulfilling your call to make disciples for Jesus Christ in these changing times. To God be the glory. Amen.

THE MAIN INGREDIENT OF A TRULY HEALTHY FAITH-BUILDING CHURCH

The main ingredient of a healthy faith-building church is for the pastor, church leaders, and the congregation to be truly born again. If you are reading this book and do not know the Lord Jesus Christ as your personal Saviour, please read the following:

1. **Accept the fact that you are a sinner, and that you have broken God's law.** The Bible says in Ecclesiastes 7:20: *"For there is not a just man upon earth that doeth good, and sinneth not."* Romans 3:23: *"For all have sinned and come short of the glory of God."*

2. **Accept the fact that there is a penalty for sin.** The Bible states in Romans 6:23: *"For the wages of sin is death..."*

3. **Accept the fact that you are on the road to hell.** Jesus Christ said in Matthew 10:28: *"And fear not them which kill the body, but are not able to kill the soul: but rather fear him which is*

able to destroy both soul and body in hell."

The Bible says in Revelation 21:8: *"But the fearful, and unbelieving, and the abominable, and murderers, and whoremongers and sorcerers, and idolaters, and all liars, shall have their part in the lake which burneth with fire and brimstone: which is the second death."*

4. **Accept the fact that you cannot do anything to save yourself!** The Bible states in Ephesians 2:8, 9: *"For by grace are ye saved through faith: and that not of yourselves: it is a gift of God. Not of works, lest any man should boast."*

5. **Accept the fact that God loves you more than you love yourself, and that He wants to save you from hell.** *"For God so loved the world, that He gave His only begotten Son, that whosoever believeth in Him should not perish, but have everlasting life"* (John 3:16).

6. With these facts in mind, please repent of your sins, believe on the Lord Jesus Christ and pray and ask Him to come into your heart and save you this very moment.

The Bible states in the book of Romans 10:9, 13: *"That if thou shalt confess with thy mouth the Lord Jesus, and shalt believe in thine heart that God hath raised Him from the dead, thou shalt be saved." "For whosoever shall call upon the name of the Lord shall be saved."*

7. If you are willing to trust Christ as your Saviour please pray with me the following prayer:

Heavenly Father, I realize that I am a sinner and that I have sinned against you. For Jesus Christ's sake, please forgive me of all of my sins. I now believe with all of my heart that Jesus Christ died, was buried, and rose again for me. Lord Jesus, please come into my heart, save my soul, change my life, and fill me with your Holy Ghost today and forever. Amen.

Introduction

1. Warren, Rick. *The Purpose Driven Church*. Zondervan Publishing House, Grand Rapids, Michigan, 1995, page 87.

Chapter 1

1. Nanus, Burt. *Visionary Leadership*. Jossey-Bass Publishers, San Francisco, 1992, page 3.
2. Miller, Craig. *NextChurch.Now*. Warner Faith, New York, New York, 2004, page 59.
3. Ibid, 59.
4. Warren, Rick. *The Purpose Driven Church*. Zondervan Publishing House, Grand Rapids, Michigan, 1995, page 87.
5. Willow Creek Associate Website, Accessed June 2008.
6. Warren, Rick. *The Purpose Driven Church*. Zondervan Publishing House, Grand Rapids, Michigan, 1995, page 100.
7. Ibid, 101.
8. Ibid, 101.
9. Miller, Craig. *NextChurch.Now*. Warner Faith, New York, New York, 2004, page 57.
10. Ibid, 58.
11. Ibid, 58.
12. MacMillan, Pat. *The Performance Factor*. Broadman and Holman Publishers, Nashville, Tennessee, 2001, page 36.
13. Ibid, 36.

14. Miller, Craig. *NextChurch.Now.* Warner Faith, New York, New York, 2004, page 70.
15. Ibid, 70.
16. Dungy, Tony. *Quiet Strength.* Tyndale House Publishers, Carol Stream Illinois, 2007, page 98.

Chapter 2

1. Stanley, Andy and Stuart Hall. *The Seven Checkpoints for Youth Leaders.* Howard Books, New York, New York, 2001, page 35.
2. Nouwen, Henri. *The Way of the Heart.* HarperOne, San Francisco, California, 1981, page 25.
3. Stanley, Andy and Stuart Hall. *The Seven Checkpoints for Youth Leaders.* Howard Books, New York, New York, 2001, page 77.
4. Ibid, 103.
5. McCain, John. *Character Is Destiny.* Random House, New York, New York, 2005, page 7.
6. Dayton, Howard. *Your Money Counts.* Tyndale House Publishers, Carol Stream, Illinois, 1997, back cover.
7. Cline, Foster and Jim Fay. *Parenting with Love and Logic.* Pinon Press, Colorado Spring, Colorado, 2006, page 24.
8. Warren, Rick. *The Purpose Driven Church.* Zondervan Publishing House, Grand Rapids, Michigan, 1995, page 31.
9. Maxwell, John. *The 21 Irrefutable Laws of Leadership.* Thomas Nelson Publishers, Nashville, Tennessee, 2002, page 25.
10. Ibid, 5.
11. Ibid, 39.
12. Ibid, 121.
13. Covey, Stephen. *First Things First.* Fireside (Simon and Schuster), New York, New York, 1994, page 37.
14. Wilkes, Gene. *Jesus On Leadership.* Tyndale House Publishers, Carol Stream, Illinois, 1998, page 18.
15. Burns, David. *Feeling Good.* Avon Books, New York, New York, 1980, page 34.
16. Ibid, 36.
17. Ibid, 37.

18. Maxwell, John. *Developing The Leaders Around You*. Thomas Nelson Publishers, Nashville, Tennessee, 1995, page 47-59.
19. Ibid, 48.
20. Ibid, 61.
21. Ibid, 84.

Chapter 3
1. Warren, Rick. *The Purpose Driven Church*. Zondervan Publishing House, Grand Rapids, Michigan, 1995, page 242.
2. Ibid, 245.
3. Ibid, 103.
4. Miller, Craig. *NextChurch.Now*. Discipleship Resources, Nashville, Tennessee, 2000, page 141.
5. Ibid, 149.
6. Troeger, Thomas. *Imagining A Sermon*. Abingdon Press, Nashville, Tennessee, 1990, page 15.

Chapter 4

1. Miller, Craig. *NextChurch.Now*. Discipleship Resources, Nashville, Tennessee, 2000, page 106.
2. Ibid, 106.
3. Ibid, 106.
4. Ibid, 106.
5. Maxwell, John. *Developing The Leaders Around You*. Thomas Nelson Publishers, Nashville, Tennessee, 1995, page 84.
6. Hybels, Bill. *Marriage: Building Real Intimacy*. Zondervan Publishing House, Grand Rapids, Michigan, 1996, page 35.

Chapter 5

1. Wilkins, Scott. *Reach: A Team Approach to Evangelism and Assimilation*. Baker Books, Grand Rapids, Michigan, 2005, page 36.
2. Warren, Rick. *The Purpose Driven Church*. Zondervan Publishing House, Grand Rapids, Michigan, 1995, page 156.
3. Ibid, 161-166.
4. Ibid, 161.

5. Ibid, 163.
6. Ibid, 165.
7. Ibid, 166.
8. Ibid, 136.
9. Ibid, 175.
10. Ibid, 190.
11. Mittelberg, Mark. *Building A Contagious Church*. Zondervan Publishing House, Grand Rapids, Michigan, 2000, page 211.
12. Ibid, 221.
13. Ibid, 224.
14. Ibid, 225.
15. Ibid, 231.
16. Ibid, 235.
17. Hybels, Bill. *Just Walk Across The Room*. Zondervan Publishing House, Grand Rapids, Michigan, 2006, page 35.
18. Ibid, 59-103.
19. Ibid, 61.
20. Ibid, 82.
21. Kimball, Dan. *They Like Jesus But Not The Church*. Zondervan Publishing House, Grand Rapids, Michigan, 2007, page 104.
22. Ibid, 112.
23. Ibid, 168.
24. Ibid, 168.

Chapter 6

1. Warren, Rick. *The Purpose Driven Church*. Zondervan Publishing House, Grand Rapids, Michigan, 1995, page 366.
2. Ibid, 368.
3. Ibid, 248.
4. Ibid, 238-239.
5. Bennis, Warren. *Organizing Genius*. Perseus Books, Cambridge, Massachusetts, 1997, page 199.
6. Ibid, 200.
7. Ibid, 198.
8. Osteen, Joel. *Your Best Life Now.* Warne Faith, New York, New York, 2004, page 3.

Chapter 7

1. Fields, Doug. *Purpose Driven Youth Ministry*. Zondervan Publishing House, Grand Rapids, Michigan, 1998, page 138.
2. Warren, Rick. *The Purpose Driven Life*. Zondervan Publishing House, Grand Rapids, Michigan, 2002, page 138.
3. Ibid, 146.
4. Ibid, 148.
5. Clifton, Donald and Paula Nelson. *Soar With Your Strengths*. Dell Publishing, New York, New York, 1992, page 134.
6. Warren, Rick. *The Purpose Driven Life*. Zondervan Publishing House, Grand Rapids, Michigan, 2002, page 141.

Bennis, Warren. *Organizing Genius*. Perseus Books, Cambridge, Massachusetts, 1997.

Burns, David. *Feeling Good*. Avon Books, New York, New York, 1980.

Clifton, Donald and Paula Nelson. *Soar With Your Strengths*. Dell Publishing, New York, New York, 1992.

Cline, Foster and Jim Fay. *Parenting with Love and Logic*. Pinon Press, Colorado Springs, Colorado, 2006.

Covey, Stephen R. *First Things First*. Fireside (Simon & Schuster), New York, New York, 1994.

Dayton, Howard. *Your Money Counts*. Tyndale House Publishers, Carol Stream, Illinois, 1997.

Dungy, Tony. *Quiet Strength*. Tyndale House Publishers, Carol Stream, Illinois, 2007.

Fields, Doug. *Purpose Driven Youth Ministry*. Zondervan Publishing House, Grand Rapids, Michigan, 1998.

Holy Bible (King James Version). Oxford University Press, New York, New York, 1967.

Holy Bible (New Revised Standard Version). Thomas Nelson Publishers, Nashville, Tennessee, 1989.

Hybels, Bill. *Just Walk Across the Room*. Zondervan Publishing House, Grand Rapids, Michigan, 2006.

Hybels, Bill. *Marriage: Building Real Intimacy*. Zondervan Publishing House, Grand Rapids, Michigan, 1996.

Kimball, Dan. *They Like Jesus But Not The Church*. Zondervan Publishing House, Grand Rapids, Michigan, 2007.

MacMillan, Pat. *The Performance Factor*. Broadman and Holman Publishers, Nashville, Tennessee, 2001.

Maxwell, John. *Developing The Leaders Around You*. Thomas Nelson Publishers, Nashville, Tennessee, 1995.

Maxwell, John. *The 21 Irrefutable Laws of Leadership*. Thomas Nelson Publishers, Nashville, Tennessee, 2002.

McCain, John. *Character Is Destiny*. Random House, New York, New York, 2005.

Miller, Craig. *NextChurch.Now*. Discipleship Resources, Nashville, Tennessee. 2000.

Mittelberg, Mark. *Building A Contagious Church*. Zondervan Publishing House, Grand Rapids, Michigan, 2000.

Nanus, Burt. *Visionary Leadership*. Jossey-Bass Publishers, San Francisco, 1992.

Nouwen, Henri. *The Way of the Heart*. HarperOne, San Francisco, California, 1981.

Osteen, Joel. *Your Best Life Now*. Warner Faith, New York, New York, 2004.

Stanley, Andy and Stuart Hall. *The Seven Checkpoints For Youth Leaders*. Howard Books, New York, New York, 2001.

Troeger, Thomas. *Imagining A Sermon*. Abingdon Press, Nashville, Tennessee, 1990.

Warren, Rick. *The Purpose Driven Church*. Zondervan Publishing House, Grand Rapids, Michigan, 1995.

Warren, Rick. *The Purpose Driven Life*. Zondervan Publishing House, Grand Rapids, Michigan, 2002.

Wilkes, C. Gene. *Jesus On Leadership*. Tyndale House Publishers, Carol Stream, Illinois, 1998.

Wilkins, Scott. *Reach: A Team Approach to Evangelism and Assimilation*. Baker Books, Grand Rapids, Michigan, 2005.

A native of the south and a graduate of the University of North Carolina at Chapel-Hill, Emory University's Candler School of Theology in Atlanta, and Colorado Theological Seminary, "Jimmy," as he likes to be called, uses a home spun, no non-sense approach to church leadership issues. He has been a pastor for fourteen years and has served churches in North Carolina, Georgia and Florida. He lives in Ponte Vedra Beach, Florida with his wife, Lynn, and their son, Caleb.

Feel free to contact him at: emory95@msn.com with any questions or concerns about your church.

Made in the USA
Columbia, SC
12 February 2025